Mayo

- The Waters and the Wild -

Paintings by John P. McHugh

Text by Michael Mullen

Cottage
Publications

First published by Cottage Publications,
an imprint of Laurel Cottage Ltd.
Donaghadee, N. Ireland 2004.
Copyrights Reserved.
© Illustrations by John P. McHugh 2004.
© Text by Michael Mullen 2004.
All rights reserved.
No part of this book may be reproduced or stored on any media
without the express written permission of the publishers.
Design & origination in Northern Ireland.
Printed & bound in Singapore.
ISBN 1 900935 40 6

The Author

Michael Mullen, novelist, short storywriter and journalist was born in Castlebar, County Mayo. He was educated in the local national school, then at Mallow and Waterford Training College before becoming a teacher in 1958 and also attended UCD.

Michael spent several years teaching in Mauritius as well as in schools in Ireland. He is also the author of some thirty books and has written extensively for children in both Irish and English. His novels include *Magus the Lollipop Man* and *The Sea Wolves from the North*. Other major fiction includes *Kelly*, *Festival of Fools*, *The Hungry Land*, *Rites of Inheritance* and *The House of Mirrors*. He deals in his writing with many aspects of Irish history and cultural identity, and is at present engaged on a major trilogy which spans the twentieth century.

He lives quietly with his wife Deirdre in Castlebar.

Best Wishes
Michael Mullen

The Artist

John Peter McHugh was born in Castlebar and has been painting with watercolours and oils since he was fifteen. Largely self taught, he has taken part in numerous group exhibitions as well as one man shows.

John is also a highly regarded tutor and often runs watercolour classes in Castlebar and Westport. Many pieces of his work has been acquired by both national and international collectors and many notable names here and abroad have been the recipients of his paintings as formal presentations.

Irish weather permitting, John frequently paints outdoors and his work thus reflects the ever-changing moods of this beautiful countryside.

He currently resides in Castlebar with his wife and family.

Best Wishes
John McHugh

Contents

Welcome to Mayo

Mayo is a varied and various county. On a geological map it looks like an irregular patchwork quilt. The diverse Mayo landscape springs from this variety of rock and soil. To the east the land is rich and fertile; to the west the coast is indented with quartzite peaks; to the north lie lonely tracts of blanket bog and great ranges of mountains mark the south. The passing clouds, fine mists and shafts of sunlight play upon this landscape changing the colours, the depths and even the distance. Sometimes the mountains are remote and firm, sometimes covered by a mystical haze and uncertainty. They are everchanging. Paul Henry and many others have caught them in all of their moods and variations.

The vast and lonely boglands stretch forever. They possess their own diverse flora and fauna which gives these boglands their subtle colours ranging from silver grey to purple and vermilion. Here and there the bogs are stippled by bog cotton, with puffy white heads while the great and silent water-pools mirror the blue skies, the moving clouds and the nocturnal stars. The silence, which lies on these bogs, is immense, broken only by the sound of migrating birds or the winds, sometimes sad, sometimes so low as to be almost indiscernible.

And while these boglands pools and lakes can be calm, the seas are almost never so. In their winter moods they are never at ease. They have a long unbroken run from the middle Atlantic and beat their hard fists against Inishturk, Clare Island, Achill Head, the lonely Iniskea Islands and Erris Head. They retreat to gather force and charge again against the headlands. In their summer moods they can be gentle and purr about the headlands with cats' paws. When the seas are silent and the sun has changed the waters to molten bronze, some believe that you can see Hy Brasil, a mystical island, shrouded in fog or lying beneath the ocean, which appears only once every seven years.

But these seas hold a sadder memory for it was on the island of Inishglora in the Bay of Erris that the Children of Lir spent the last three hundred years of their lives. It is the saddest of tales. Here buffeted by the winter gales and the wild seas they were swept apart and almost lost until eventually they reached the Island of the Seals. On that lonely island the four swans made music and sang together with none but the seals to listen to them. It is a strange poignant story stirring the heart at many levels.

In more recent times Yeats, meeting Synge in Paris, directed him to travel to the Aran Islands *"to express a life that has never found expression"*. Synge turned from his study of the French language and began to write a series of plays based on Irish themes and the most famous perhaps is *The Playboy of the Western World*. While it was filled with majestic poetry and Christy Mahon, Peen Mike and the Widow Quinn are substantial characters full of Celtic vitality and life it was not received with enthusiasm at the Abbey Theatre – in fact it caused a famous riot. It did not sit well with the nationalists who were forging a new state and sought Celtic perfection in its population. Indeed they considered *Playboy* a travesty of western Irish life evoking a peasantry of alcoholics and ineffectual fantasists rather than a people ready to assume the responsibilities of self-government. But it has outlasted the criticism and still plays to packed houses.

Pagan or Christian, Croagh Patrick is a sacred mountain. It rises like a pyramid from the southern shores of Clew Bay and there is a pilgrim way like a white glistening cicatrise on its flank. It has been worn white by the feet of pilgrims and is as sacred to us as Mount Fujiyama is to the Japanese. Day after day, year after year the pilgrims make their way up this path seeking out the austere inspiration sought by Saint Patrick who spent forty days on this quartzite peak. There is a small church on the summit and on Reek Sunday people move about this church as if they were part of a great prayer wheel, calling out in rhythmic supplication.

Croagh Patrick has attracted pilgrims, writers and poets all through the generations. At its base are the ruins of Murrisk Abbey, an Augustinian foundation dating from 1457. Perhaps what we remember most concerning this seat of learning is William Bourke's poem *The Friar's Farewell to Murrisk*. He loved his abbey in sight of the sacred mountain. He wrote,

"Farewell to lovely Murrisk. So beautiful so fair
Encircled with great mountains
On each side of the bay."

A priest, who in Irish is called *An Caisideach Bán* or Fair Cassidy, wrote a more intense poem. He was torn between his love for the church and for a woman. Above all he is honest about his searing emotions:

'I left my prayers and the kneeling pilgrims
And went wild running down the Holy Reek
And all who saw me said; "That is Cassidy
Who abandoned God for a girl's cheek"
I have no land, no stock, nor money
To win that girl to me, I cannot pray,
But I'd mount the Reek on my bleeding knees
If I could have her on my wedding day.'

Below the northern slopes of Croagh Patrick lies Clew Bay and set on on its eastern edge stands Westport House. Richard Cassels designed the house with additions and alterations made by James Wyatt. The house is at the edge Westport town, a picturesque, planned town where tree-lined streets run by the river giving the whole scene an open and urban quality.

The eastern road from the town leads to Ballintubber Abbey. Once partly derelict it has now been restored to some of its former beauty. The abbey itself was founded in 1216 and religious services have been carried out since its foundation. It is interesting for many reasons not least for its Roman and Gothic arches where the two styles are in harmony rather than in conflict. There is a pilgrim path here called *Tóchar Phádraig* which leads to Croagh Patrick and it is said Carolan the Harper passed this abbey on his way to entertain at Castleburke.

Not far along the road one comes upon one of Mayo's most famous houses – Moore Hall. Each generation made its mark upon its history, but the name we most associate with it is George Moore, whose influence on James Joyce was quite considerable. It stands on Muckloon Hill overlooking Lough Carra, which Moore made famous in his novel *The Lake*. In fact it could be regarded as the most famous literary lake in the world. In wonderfully turned phrases Moore begins,

'It was one of those enticing days at the beginning of May when white clouds are drawn about the earth like curtains. The lake lay like a mirror that someone had breathed upon, the brown islands showing through the mist faintly, with grey shadows falling into the water, blurred at the edges. The ducks were talking softly in the reeds, the reeds themselves were talking; and the water lapped softly about the smooth limestone shores.'

It ends with these magical, evocative lines,

'On the deck of the steamer he heard the lake's warble above the violence of the waves. "There is a lake in every man's heart," he said, clinging to a wet rope; he added, "And every man must ungird his loins for the crossing."'

Perhaps Ireland's most underrated writer, Moore wrote one of the most accomplished autobiographies in the English language, *Hail and Farewell*. His cremated remains are interred on Castle Island.

The road from Moore Hall takes one to Ballinrobe and then to the delightful village of Cong. The Kings of Connaught richly endowed its abbey and many of their royal relations are buried there close to the pleasant tree-shaded river. One of the treasures at the National Museum is the processional Cross of Cong, made from gold filigree, gilt bronze and gems. On the side of this gracious cross are written the words *"In this cross is preserved the cross on which the founder of the world suffered"*. The abbey itself is a medieval treasure with its fine stone carvings on windows, cloisters and doorways and the work of the Cong school of carvers can be found in many other religious sites around Connaught. Cong is surrounded by water and is close to Loughs Mask and Corrib. These magical lakes are connected and fed by rivers which flow underground, for beneath the land lie limestone caves, mysterious tunnels and waterways.

Cross the river bridge and you are in the beautiful demesne of Ashford Castle built for Sir Arthur Edward Guinness. It is close to the shore of Lough Corrib, and is used in the opening shot of *The Quiet Man*. Some wit has said that it was the only cowboy film every shot outside Hollywood. The filming of *The Quiet Man* in June 1951 changed the village and the area forever. It was the first time that American audiences saw the beauty of Western Ireland in colour and each year the

tourists arrive at the village to see the sights made famous by the film and try and live some of the magic of that time.

Cong is always tranquil and there is always the whisper of water to be heard as it flows over some weir or other. The area surrounding Cong is marked by many cairns, stone circles, ring forts, standing stones, souterrains and passage graves. Close by is where Sir William Wilde, the father of Oscar, built his house in 1865. He was an accomplished archaeologist and called the house Moytura as it was reputed to be the site of the famous battle of Moytura. Joy Melville, the biographer of Oscar's mother, wrote,

'There is the same sense of peace around Moytura House today that must have attracted William Wilde over a century ago. Great lakes are all around; even the market town of Cong is full of water gushing out of rocks and bubbling up in pools to form the River Cong.'

This landscape, with its beauty and Celtic memory, must have had a formative influence upon the future playwright. He would have heard his father speak of the fairy-lore, the folklore, the mythology and the archaeology of the area.

On the road to the Ballinrobe lies the Neale. Here in this pleasant limestone landscape are to be found many interesting archaeological sites. It was the Parish Priest of the Neale, Father O'Malley, who introduced the word boycott into the language. It derives its name from Captain Charles Cunningham Boycott who was land agent for the Earl of Erne. Because the labourers refused to work for him he had to import labour from the north of Ireland and a thousand soldiers were employed to protected these labourers. The event received widespread media coverage. He was not the worst of men, but he was severe and rigid and would not compromise. The people in the area offered passive resistance and he left. This silent protest has had worldwide repercussions particularly in India.

Beyond Claremorris lies the village of Knock which attracts pilgrims from all over the world. They visit the Marian shrine, the scene of a silent apparition in 1879. More than a million people visit this shrine every year. The tall spire of the cathedral rises like a beacon above the flat countryside, like the many round towers of Mayo which must have guided pilgrims towards a safe haven in the early Christian Church, for Mayo abounds in these magnificent structures.

Knock airport is close by and as we say, 'Father Horan raised us up on the back of eagle's wings', when, in the face of huge obstacles he had this airport built. Each year it spreads its air routes further into Europe and brings London and other great cities to within an hour of this remote area.

The Moy drains north Mayo. This winding river is like a blue membrane on the land. A gentle river never given to dramatic moods, the Moy is never angry and it never complains. It is a salmon river and greatly loved by fishermen who stand silently on its banks hour after hour waiting for the elusive fish. Beginning tentatively in Sligo, close to the Ox Mountains, it is fed by a myriad of tributaries until it has become a wide river as it passes Ballina and opens into the Moy Estuary. It brings together a great network of lakes and rivers and binds the whole expansive area into a geographical unity.

Along the Moy Rivers banks you will find mountains and boglands, small towns and villages, great abbeys now in ruins and castles with watchful turrets. The river passes through both busy bustling towns and through lonely places sometimes visited only by the reflection of stars. To pass down this river is in many ways to be a witness to the history and geography of all Mayo.

This symmetrical mountain rises from the southern shores of Clew Bay. It possesses a quartzite core and was once the heart of a much higher mountain but time and weather have worn its soft covering away. It stands firmly on the horizon and is a symbol for the county. On a summer's evening it is a dark silhouette on the skyline. In summer, when the sun plays upon its flanks the colour runs from grey to light purple to deep purple.

Along its back and spine runs a pilgrim path worn bright by the feet of pilgrims. Even before Saint Patrick spent forty days and nights upon its summit there was a pilgrim path leading from the royal seat at Rath Cruachain in Roscommon to its summit and the feast of Lughnasa was celebrated there before the early Christians imposed a new pilgrimage upon an ancient one.

Today part of this ancient pilgrim path has been opened up and reinstated. The path is called *Tóchar Phádraig* and leads from Ballintubber Abbey to the top of the sacred mountain. A small chapel now stands at the summit of the Reek as we like to call the historic remains, and on Pilgrim Sunday masses of people move about it chanting prayer as if they were part of a great sacred wheel.

Each day and in all weathers there is someone making a pilgrimage to the top of Croagh Patrick. They seek out the thin place of Celtic spirituality, where there is a fine partition between the sacred and profane.

Writers and artists alike have been drawn to this religious place. H.V. Morton in his travel book *In Search of Ireland* writes of the moment when he reached the summit,

'I went inside and knelt down. The place was very small and ice cold. A young priest knelt in prayer. The wind howled round the little building in soft gusts, and I wondered what it felt like to be there in the great storms that swept in from the Atlantic… I was conscious that, outside, the mountain mists were sweeping past; the cold air told of a remote solitude; the rudeness of the little sanctuary was that of a shrine built on the outpost of the world. The kneeling priest never moved. He might have been carved of stone. He reminded me of some knight keeping vigil before the altar.'

Croagh Patrick

John P. Mc Hugh

This lake is set between steep-sided mountains. At their bases lies scree, which has been dislodged by ice, wind and changing weather. Translated from the Irish it means Dark Lake. On calm days, when the lake is like a mirror, it carries the images of the high mountains. It is a lonely, brooding place and comfort is brought to the eye by the presence of some trees at the end of the lake.

It is a place of spare and austere beauty and a great tranquillity and peace lies about. However if the tourist stops at the end of the lake to take photographs, they may notice the rough unevenly shaped cross which recalls the tragic event which occurred there during the famine. In the spring of 1847, the potato having failed, six hundred starving people made their way to Delphi Lodge in order to apply to the board of guardians for food. At Louisburgh many had already perished. The rest had to cross the Glankeen River, which was in full flood, in order to reach Delphi. Wet and cold they reached the hunting lodge and while the guardians continued with their dinner they sat on the ground and waited. When they were refused relief or tickets, they began the return journey to Louisburgh. It was a bitterly cold night and when they reached a high place called Stroppabue the wind was blowing so hard that many were blown off the cliff to fall to their deaths in the lake beneath. The stone cross recalls this tragic event.

Further down the lake and towards the south is Delphi Fishing Lodge. The name Delphi sounds out of place in such a remote area but it was so named by the Marquis of Sligo had been on a tour of Greece and on his return the place reminded him of Delphi in Greece, hence its unusual name. The Lodge now belongs to Peter and Jane Mantle and this Victorian Fishing Lodge, once the property of the Marquis of Sligo, is now one of the best fly-fishing locations in Ireland.

Doo Lough

Achill is a dramatic island, with its sheer cliffs, its towering mountain, its various weather and the thundering seas which beat about it.

At its eastern end it is joined to the mainland by a bridge at Achill Sound and Slievemore or 'The Great Mountain' composed of quarts and mica rises abruptly from the ocean. At the western end of the island, Croaghaun Mountain drops into the sea as if part of the island had sheered off and disappeared.

Once Achill was famous for its amethyst, and amethyst stones are still familiar on the island. Its varied and interesting geology has drawn many geologists to the island over the years. The most famous of these was Robert Lloyd Praeger. He wrote,

'Achill, wind-swept and bare, heavily peat-covered, with great gaunt brown mountains rising here and there, and a wild coast hammered by the Atlantic on all sides but the east, has a strange charm which everyone feels, but no one can fully explain.'

History has left its mark on the area. Evidence of the original farmers can still be found in the landscape as at the Céide Fields. Neolithic tombs and cairns are found all over the island at every corner and cove reminders of past history can be found.

When the fuchsia and rhododendron bloom in late spring/early summer the island is awash with colour. Artists and writers have been drawn here over the years. Paul Henry arrived on Achill in 1910 for a brief visit and remained seven years in which time he painted perhaps the most famous and memorable paintings of the island. Today Camille Souter, arguably one of the finest artists of her generation, lives at Keel.

Heinrich Böll, the German Nobel prizewinner, was drawn to this island and wrote a book *An Irish Diary* describing his visit. His house is now known as the Heinrich Böll Centre. It lies beside Doogort village and has become a literary and artistic centre. It is a vital place where writers and artists hold residencies. Among other names of note, the poet John Dean was born on Achill and Paul Durcan is a frequent visitor to the island.

The easily accessed strand at Keel is long and lovely, however you have to travel across a precipitous mountain road to reach the even more picturesque strand at Keem. Whichever they choose, for the visitor, Achill is a perfectly contained place and one of the finest holiday destinations in Ireland.

Achill Island

In Irish it is known as *Barna Na Gaoithe* – the Gap of the Wind as the wind is funnelled through here from the western flatlands beneath. Holding a commanding view of Nephin and the mountains, from the halting spot here you can observe the whole western landscape of Mayo. Below are small farms and pockets of sweet land and in the distance, Lough Conn stretches down in the direction of Crossmolina – one gets a true sense of the grandeur of the Mayo landscape from this, The Windy Gap.

Nephin Mountain, shaped like the back of a great whale, is the highest mountain in Mayo and is formed from Dalradian quartzite. Its slopes carry deep ridges like great grey slashes and from its summit one can see into three counties.

On stormy days the wind has a sad voice as it forces its way through the gap. The land is poor and boggy here and the purple heather adds muted colour to the surroundings. The road is well tarred and takes one from Castlebar through an elevated landscape through the gap and down into Crossmolina.

It was through this gap that the French soldiers and the Irish insurgents in their great coats made their way on the eve of the Races of Castlebar. It was a night of dramatic weather. The rain fast falling heavily, thunder rattled overhead and lightning flashed in forks across the night sky. Laboriously they pulled the gun and gun carriage up the muddy track and through the gap. With the coming of first light they were on their way to Castlebar and their place in history.

The beauty of The Windy Gap is austere and quiet and on a summer day when the shafts of sunlight break through the moving clouds, the landscape is wonderful to behold. The air is always fresh and invigorating at the entrance to this gap in the mountains.

Nephin

John P McHugh

This great building, firm and resolute, stands upon a sacred site. In the distance stands the symmetrically-shaped mountain of Saint Patrick, The Reek or Croagh Patrick and it is said that the Saint founded the original church at Ballintubber in 441 AD after his return from his forty-day fast on the summit of the sacred mountain.

Built of limestone, Ballintubber is a symbol of continuity and certitude in religious belief. This great abbey, where both Roman and Gothic architecture meet, belongs to a confident civilisation and was built by King Cathal O'Connor in 1216 for the Canon regulars of Saint Augustine.

It has an austere dignity and is unfettered by exuberant ornament. Its white-walled interior, with timber beams and sturdy stone arches, preside over a dignified piety.

Close by is *Tóchar Phádraig* or the Pilgrim's walk. Pilgrims on their way west rested at the abbey on their way to the Reek. On their return the pilgrims washed their feet in the bathhouse after their long journey. This bathhouse is called *Dabhach an Chóra* – The Bath of the Righteous.

Ballintubber is a living place. It is a religious storehouse and draws people from all over the world. We leave this abbey knowing that the spiritual side of our nature has been exercised.

It was built by a king, made saintly by pilgrims, desecrated by Cromwellian soldiers in 1653, endured the Penal Laws, lay in piteous half-ruins for many years and then emerged from the grey ashes of history. Recently Brother Joseph McNally, who was born in Ballintubber and founded the art college in Singapore, donated the statue of Our Lady of Ballintubber just inside the main gate. His sculpture of Saint Patrick bending over a sacred well is beyond the abbey boundary and, to the east, standing amid the reeds of Lough Carra, stands his magnificent figure of Christ waiting for the fishermen to return from the lake. This was his final testament to his native place.

Ballintubber has endured all that history can inflict upon it. It has had its splendid times, its dark ruinous times, times when hope was feeble and it has had its resurrection. It stands today firm and pristine and is a symbol to endurance and faith.

Ballintubber Abbey

John P Mc Hugh

This green area, defined by trees and bound by chains should be known as The Green but locals call it The Mall. It was set out and defined by Lord Lucan and has the feel of an English green, a feel which must have been even stronger when officers from the Military barracks once played cricket here. A path runs through it and about it.

The real Mall is at the end of the Green: a covered path, straight as an arrow and leading to the firm and imposing Protestant Church standing half way up Mountain View. Lord Lucan and his family could walk directly from their home called the Lawn to the Church without being interrupted or observed by the general population.

The Binghams developed Castlebar and it has always been the centre of administration for the county. The town takes its name from Barry's Castle, which stood where the Military Barracks now stands.

The buildings around the Mall are testament to the changing course of Mayo History and indeed to stand at the centre of the Mall or the Green is to observe the history of Castlebar in stone.

An imposing courthouse, with a Greek façade and heavy Doric pillars testified to its serious intent. After the 1798 rebellion heavy sentences were imposed upon the insurgents and many of them were hanged from the hanging tree, which stood close to the Presbyterian Church and almost opposite Daly's Hotel.

John Wesley preached in the Church on his tour of Ireland and at Daly's Hotel, Michael Davitt and James Daly, editor of the *Connaught Telegraph*, founded the Land League in August 1895.

Beside the courthouse a plaque marks the house in which Margaret Burke Sheridan was born on the 15th October 1889. She was born with a golden voice, was educated at Eccles Street and eventually went to London and Italy to train as a soprano. She was the great diva of her day and made her debut singing Mimi in *La Bohème*. She was well loved by the Italian audiences, especially when she sang in *Madame Butterfly*. In 1936 she retired suddenly and took up residence in the Shelbourne Hotel. She died in Dublin in 1985.

The Mall, Castlebar

John P. Mc Hugh

The lordly Moy passes through Ballina before opening gently into Killala Bay on its final journey to the sea. The Moy is famous for its salmon fisheries and the most famous place of all is The Ridge Pool to which fishermen come from all over the world.

The historic roots of Ballina are ancient and it is a waterway into the heartland of Mayo. Ballina, as the name indicates, is at a river ford. It had links with the earliest settlers in Mayo, for not only are there Céide fields to the west but cultivated fields have also been discovered in Glencree to the east. Beside the railway station stands the Dolmen of the Four Maols. This fine dolmen is said to mark the final resting place of the four foster brothers of King Guaire. At his bequest they murdered the rightful heir to the Kingship of Connaught and were executed for their deed.

There are the ruins of many monastic foundations in the locality and Saint Olcán founded a church in the area. Ballina belongs to the Kilmoremoy parish which is derived from Irish meaning 'The Great Church of the

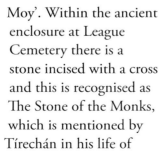

Moy'. Within the ancient enclosure at League Cemetery there is a stone incised with a cross and this is recognised as The Stone of the Monks, which is mentioned by Tírechán in his life of Saint Patrick. Across the river can be seen the slightly submerged ruins of the Augustinian Friary founded in 1427.

Lord Tyrawley founded modern Ballina in 1723 when he introduced a large number of skilled flax and linen workers to the town. However the linen industry lasted but for a short time and the tranquil life of Ballina was interrupted by the arrival of Humbert who made himself master of the town in August 1798. Ballina expanded early in the nineteenth century when the Ham Bridge with its five arches was built across the river and the Moy itself was tamed and ordered by the building of strong walls along its banks. Ships were brought down Killala Bay to the town. Between 1830 and 1842 there was a housing boom in the town and Georgian façades replaced the old buildings.

One of its most distinguished citizens in recent years is Mary Robinson who was elected the first woman President of Ireland in 1990. In 1997 she took up an appointment as United Nations Commissioner for Human Rights.

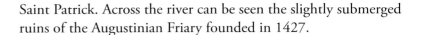

River Moy, Ballina

Everyone with a sensitive eye stops at Pontoon Bridge and studies the waters of Lough Conn running into Lough Cullen where there is always a hopeful fisherman waiting patiently for a fish. On misty days the distance is foreshortened and mysterious, on bright days, the definition of mountain and wood precise. In the western distance Mount Nephin stands in a lordly position above the lake. When the waters are in flood they are querulous, at other times the waters are as even as a mirror and reflect the passing clouds. It can be moody and melancholic on rainy days, airy and fresh on clear days.

The islands in front of Pontoon Bridge Hotel have the delicate appearance that one associates with Japanese screen painting. They are set artfully on the water and fringed with delicate bushes and small trees. Here and there the hard granite breaks the skin of these islands.

It is said that there was once a pontoon bridge here before the first permanent bridge was built and this is where the name is derived, but it sounds too easy. I prefer the less obvious explanation that it is derived from *Bun Dá Abhainn*, which means 'the bottom of the two rivers'.

A stylised steel engraving, executed in 1842, exists of the bridge. This engraving is filled with the romantic longings of the time. At the left edge some tourists look down from the ledge upon a stylised landscape. A huddle of thatched houses lies beyond the bridge and dreamy sailing boats ply across still waters. In the middle distance there is the road and the curved bridge bearing the people and traffic of the day.

Pontoon Bridge still retains some of that romantic longing associated with the first half of the nineteenth century.

Pontoon

John P McHugh

Turlough means dry lake although there is no dry lake in evidence there. A dainty tower beside the ruins of a seventeenth century church dominates the area. Two stone crucifixions, one above the entrance door and the other above one of the windows, possess a lonely and primitive quality one finds in penal crosses.

There has been constant habitation in this area as is evidenced by the raths, which dominate the hills and the *fulachta fiadha*, which are found in abundance here. The land runs in small hillocks to the west and in the east, opens out over a spacious and wooded valley.

On a platform over a river and water meadow stands Turlough House, the former home of the Fitzgeralds who settled here on wide estates in the mid sixteenth century. Thomas Fitzgerald built the eighteenth century house just inside the gates of what is now the entrance to the Turlough Folk Museum. The new house was set on a higher level and designed by James Dean in 1886. This new house, not unlike a French chateau, has a symmetrical façade, high-pitched roofs and dormers and to the side is a service wing.

Having served many generations of Fitzgeralds, Mayo County Council purchased it in 1991. A magnificent modern folk museum was built at a lower level and adjacent to the house. The façade of the new museum is clad in white granite. When caught by light the whole building glows. This museum has exceeded all expectation and people from all over the world now visit it.

There is another Georgian house close by, now in ruins, set amongst the woods called Charleville House built by another Fitzgerald, Charles Lionel. The most famous or infamous of all the Fitzgeralds was George Robert (1748–86), who grew up to be known as the 'Fighting Fitzgerald'. He was known to bring a bear about with him to terrorize people. He was eventually executed in Castlebar although he had to be hanged twice as the rope broke on the first jump.

Turlough is a quiet village. At present a housing estate is being built close by, symptomatic of the changes taking place in Mayo. High on Turlough Hill the Fitzgeralds repose in the family vaults beside the Round Tower.

Turlough

Lough Conn joins Lough Cullin at Pontoon bridge. Many rivers and small streams feed it before it, in turn, joins the winding Moy.

It is an artist's lake, a writer's lake but above all it is a fisherman's lake. It draws fishermen from all over Ireland and the best fishermen's tales are to be heard but not always believed at Tommy Healy's Hotel or at the Pontoon Bridge Hotel. Close to Tommy Healy's Hotel are small woods of ancient oak, magical and mossed. A different clock measures time here. Reeds grow along the shore, buff and stiff and in the winds they rub dryly against each other.

All about this lake, hidden in small woods and neat coves, are secure and private houses where those who wish to fish and have time for contemplation live. The former President of Ireland, Mary Robinson, has purchased a home close to the lake set in quiet woods on a peninsula.

Near the shore of Lough Cullin are small granite islands with intimate feathery woods. Amongst the many who retired here and led an active life in retirement was Emily McManus who wrote the autobiography *Matron of Guy's*. She fished the lake and kept her poultry and was generally happy.

Like many before her she fished for the famous brown trout and salmon as has many a fisherman after her. Anglers find their way to this place of singular beauty through Knock Airport – you can breakfast in London and by noon you are fishing on the lake. If lucky you may have your own trout served to you at one of the hotels that evening.

Lough Conn is presided over by the grandeur of Nephin Mountain with its steep polished flanks fine as dolphin skin. At the very end of the lake is Crossmolina, set on the River Deel, it is an active town. The whole area is full of historical interest. The monks built their monasteries here and Enniscoe House is now a heritage and genealogical centre.

Lough Conn

John P. McHugh

The town of Newport is the gateway to North Mayo. You arrive at Newport from Castlebar, along a long and sometimes lonely road, to be greeted at the entrance to Newport by the great railway aqueduct spanning the river with high arches. It is an imposing testament to Victorian engineering. Thomas Wynne of Castlebar, one of the finest photographers of his time, has a photograph of its construction, with the timber arches still in place.

The Medlycott family established the town in the eighteenth century. It was an active town well sustained by a linen industry supervised by immigrant Quakers. The O'Donel family took over the Medlycott estate in the late eighteenth century and built Newport House, standing above the harbour.

The great manuscript *The Battler*, better know as *The Cathach*, was rediscovered in Newport House in the early nineteenth century. *The Cathach* is the oldest surviving Irish manuscript and is attributed to *Colum Cille*. He had copied it from a manuscript belonging to his old teacher Saint Finnian. This gave rise to the first judgement on copyright ever handed down. The High King passed down the sentence, *'Le gach boin a boinín. Le gash leabhar a macleabhar'* which translated means *'To every cow belongs the calf and to every book its copy.'*

Here is a description of the rediscovery of the book as written by Sir William Bentham in 1811,

"The contents were found to be a rude wooden box, very much decayed, enclosing a MS or vellum, a copy of the ancient vulgate translation of the psalms, in Latin ... It was so much injured by damp as to appear almost a solid mass; by steeping it in cold water I was enabled to separate the membranes from each other, and by pressing each separately between blotting paper, and frequently renewing the operation, at length succeeded in restoring, what was not actually decayed, to a legible state."

It was, as we say, a close run thing.

Thanks to the upturn of our economic fortunes there is a new life now in Newport, but the town still holds its charming architectural integrity.

Newport

John P McHugh

Leave Westport and take the turning for Clifden. On your right hand lies Croagh Patrick now observed from a different angle and buttressed by high and rugged hills. These hills are wooded on the slopes and here and there a house is set amongst the trees.

Eric Cross spent the final years of his life here in Sonia Kelly's delightful Georgian house. He was born in Newry and was the author of one of the most entertaining books on folklore entitled *The Tailor and Ansty*. Eric Cross was a kind, pleasant gentleman and hugely intellectual. In his narrow room, which was as narrow as a hallway, he often showed me his inventions. They were hugely original and it was rumoured that he had worked on the Manhattan Project and that his mathematical calculations were flown from Shannon to Los Alamos. He now reposes in the small chapel at Knappagh, which is a wayside Protestant Church on the way to Clifden and an unknown lady often lays flowers upon his grave.

After Knappagh you leave the comfort of the small hills and the small woods and the land expands into bog. In the distance are the Partry Mountains, which run in a southwest direction towards Leenaun Harbour, a deep fiord that could accommodate the British navy. The Erriff River flows between the Partry Mountains and the Sheeffry Hills and Mweelrea Mountains to the north, running through bogland and moorland. It is quiet in summer but in winter the mountain streams charge it with raging water.

All along the river are fishing beats carefully measured out. Lonely fishermen stand in the mists and the sunshine, in hopeful expectation of a good fish. It is an area of rugged beauty and changing skycaps. Turf is still cut here and stacks of turf line the road. High on the mountainside sheep graze quietly. An ancient Irish oak forest still holds on tenaciously here beside the river and is some five thousand years old. High on these mountains lie undisturbed veins of metal, including gold.

The Erriff

John P McHugh

This stately house is now an imposing ruin. It was burned in 1923 but in a sense it refuses to die. The former life within this house is recalled in letters, memoirs and above all, in the works of the novelist George Moore (1852–1933). His ashes lie on Castle Island.

Moore Hall was built on Spanish gold. The first George Moore founded the fortunes of the family and he built his house overlooking Lough Carra with its many islands. He went blind in his sleep and wept that he could not enjoy the serene lake and the sight of the Partry Mountains.

His son John was caught up in the rebellious fever of the time and he rushed to join Humbert when he arrived at Castlebar. Humbert appointed him President of Connaught but after the failed rebellion he was captured. He was later to die in Waterford and his remains now rest at the corner of The Mall in Castlebar.

George Moore the second was a more sedate and remote character. A man with a sad caste of mind he wrote of Moore Hall

'beautiful as it is and as much as I love it I have not always been able to exclude ennui from its precincts.'

The third George Moore was a man of outstanding talents. As a youth he made the con-tinental tour, returning to Ireland and to Moore Hall to assume his responsibilities. A famous racehorse called Corunna won the Chester Cup for Moore which brought him £10,000 through side bets. The money was well used and some of it set aside to help tenants through the worst years of the famine. Later he became a politician and was very successful as an orator. He returned to Moore Hall on Good Friday 1870 and died soon after.

George Moore, the novelist, registered a vow that he would never do anything to deserve a popular funeral. He went to Paris, studied painting but discovered that he had only a minor talent. He began to write and at this he was an outstanding success. He produced more than sixty titles and in January 1933 he gave up a work on *A Communication to My Friends*, saying, *'I have written enough,'* and died a few days later.

The great and the good visited Moore Hall in their day, amongst them Maria Edward and Oscar Wilde. It now stands, an empty husk, as a monument to the Moore family.

Moore Hall

Lough Carra runs in to Lough Mask. The derivation of Lough Mask is open to opinion. It can mean either *The Lake Between* or *The Confused Lake* and you are free to choose.

Towns and village ring Lough Mask, which serve the many fishermen well. To the north lies Partry and southward from that is Toormakeady where Irish is still spoken. Continuing along the ring of the lake one can visit Finny, Clonbur and Ballinrobe. Ballinrobe is built on the Robe River and has developed around a seventh century church built there. It has always been a good market town and a garrison town from the early nineteenth century until 1922.

This is how Richard Aylward describes the rise of the mayfly over the lake,

> *'Ah, tis great time in this part of the world when the Mayfly rises. And isn't it curious too, the Mayfly has hardly any mouth and no jaws at all? Isn't that a curious thing? But then the creature had no need of food, and no need of any jaws or mouth to eat it, for it only lives for a few hours at the most, and that brief ecstatic existence is all filled with love-making and the delirious business of the whirling intoxication of the nuptial flight.'*

It is a lake of many islands and a place of great beauty. The road south takes you high into the mountains past Maumtrasna and on into Galway and the spectacular Joyce country.

This remote and rugged landscape carries its dark secrets for it was here, against the backdrop of mountains and close to the lake that a brutal tale unfolded. On 17th August 1882 John Joyce of Maumtrasna, his wife, his daughter, his son and his mother were all savagely murdered in a crime which shocked the country and is still set in folk memory. Several people were arrested but a terrible miscarriage of justice took place and an innocent man was hanged and four innocent men were jailed for life. Jarlath Waldron who had written a book on the matter and has studied the case makes clear that the deeper one delves into this particular case the deeper it gets, for one is dealing with raw and primitive human nature.

Lough Mask

John P. Mc Hugh

Delphi seems a strange Grecian name for an area on the remote west of Ireland. It does have a tentative Greek connection. It once belonged to the second Marquis of Sligo. He visited Greece on the grand tour and he fell so much in love with it that he wished to live there. Affairs of the estate made him return to Westport. Like all gentlemen of the time it was the custom not only to possess an estate but also to have a hunting lodge. So he built his lodge in this remote landscape and because the mountainous area reminded him so much of Delphi he called it by that name and the name has held to this day.

He tired of the lodge and during the nineteenth and early twentieth century the lodge and fisheries were let to tenants. When the lease ran out, Alec Wallace took it over. This is T. C. Kingsmill Moore's description of life at the lodge under the stewardship of Alec,

'Delphi Lodge was a big rambling house built round three sides of a square, rather dilapidated, not very comfortable or well furnished, insufficient bathrooms. Not one of these things mattered for the old house inhaled kindness and welcome. The regular frequenters were a mixed grill, a couple of civil servants from Northern Ireland, some businessmen and the whole gamut of the professions. At Delphi there was not a bar of any kind, only a press filled with every kind of drink and a child's exercise book for guests to enter their consumption.'

When he passed away a paradise had been lost.

Paradise was regained in the presence of Peter Mantle and his wife who restored it to its former splendour and then restored it some more. It is now Ireland's most famous Victorian Fishing Lodge. The fishery runs for six miles through the beautiful valley. Everywhere there is the sound of gentle water falling or splashing around this remote area. There is always some fisherman in his waterproof jacket sitting hopefully in a boat and casting his line across ruffled water.

Its remote location and remote beauty has drawn fishermen and artists from all over Europe. Life is lived here at a pace which is both relaxing and untroubled.

Delphi

John P. McHugh

The road from Newport to Mallaranny skirts the northern edge of Clew Bay and the views are both panoramic and delightful.

Along this road, some two miles from the town, is Burrishoole Abbey. Set pleasantly above a small bay, this Dominican friary was founded by Richard Burke of Turlough. In 1446 he retired to the peace and tranquillity of the cloisters and died. The beautiful de Burgo – O'Malley Chalice at the national museum belonged to this friary.

Close by, Ernie O'Malley spent many years of his life at Burrishoole Lodge. He spent his time farming, collecting folklore in this area and photographing early Irish monuments. His autobiographical works, *On Another Man's Wound* gives an account of his career in the IRA during the Anglo-Irish war. *The Singing Flame* concerns his involvement in the Civil War. Another book *Raids and Rallies* is a collection of his journalistic work. After the civil war he went to America and married Helen Hooker Roelofs, who became a successful sculpturess. Between them they built up a wonderful collection of art which was bestowed on Irish Galleries. Peter Grant's bronze sculpture of Manannan Mac Lir on Castlebar Mall was commissioned by Helen Hooker Roelofs and gifted to the town.

Rosturk Castle, which was built in the 1870s, has a strong profile amongst the woods and looks in outline like an English Medieval Castle. However, it was neither knight nor baron who built Rosturk Castle but Robert Vesey Stoney, a railway engineer. Robert Vasey Stoney had been to India and had built railways there. The drawing rooms, looking towards the sea, are based on railway arches and the chimneypiece in the dining room is believed to be from the East. There is a boathouse on the shore which was a prefab for the railway workers. He belonged to that group of magnificent engineers who fuelled the great Railway Age.

The railway, which arrived at Mallaranny in 1894, opened up the west to tourists and a great hotel with an imposing façade was built there in 1897. In its day it had every Victorian convenience: electric lights, hot and cold water baths and splendid dining facilities.

This glory has passed but as the gateway to both Achill and the Corraun Peninsula, Mallaranny is again filled with vitality.

ROSTURK

You are familiar with Ashford Castle, indeed the whole world is familiar with Ashford Castle as it features in the opening shot of the film *The Quiet Man*. Now used as a hotel, it stands on the edge of Lough Corrib and is an imposing structure with its turrets, crenulations, parapets, gables and galleries. It is as indulgent in ornament within as without. Despite the fact that it has been added to over the years it is still pleasing to the eye and sits well in its location of trees, gardens and shrubs. A limestone bridge, guarded by dainty towers, leads across a gentle river to the hotel proper. It is a statement in stone and a fairytale entrance to the main building.

It has drawn personalities from every walk of life to it. The top of the long list begins with Maureen O'Hara and ends with Barry Fitzgerald. In between is everyone else, prime ministers, stars, American senators, writers, great beauties and the scions of Royal Houses.

But Cong is greater than *The Quiet Man*. Cong is a place where you hear the gentle sound of water. The water runs over limestone beds and it is known to disappear underground for beneath Cong is a labyrinth of caves. The woods about Cong soften sound and there is never a sense of hurry in the area.

The monks were the first to appreciate the beauty of the area for Saint Feichin of Fore founded a monastery in the vicinity in the sixth century. The O'Connor family founded the twelfth century Cong Abbey whose great glory is the Cross of Cong. The exqui-site cross belongs to the same century and is amongst the great masterpieces of Irish medieval art. At the centre of the cross is enshrined a portion of the True Cross which came from Rome in 1119 and inscribed in Irish on a side of the cross is,

In this cross is preserved the cross on which the founder of the world suffered and pray for Turlough O'Conor, King of Ireland, and Abbot O'Duffy, and for the artist Maol Iosa O'Echan.

The remains of the fine abbey remind one of its ecclesiastical importance in former times.

Ashford Castle

This headland projects into Clew Bay on the southern coast opposite Mallaranny. Consisting of twin hills covered with delicate woods of hazel, silver birch and many other trees, at its base is a pier jutting out into the sea in a confident manner, possessing an intimate and private atmosphere. The beach has been improved and extended and one can walk for miles along the seashore.

Close by is Old Head Hotel. It was justly famous in its time because of a single family and a singular personality – Alec Wallace. His story and his achievements are worthy of telling. He was knowledgeable on most things, had a singular interest in learning and very little interest in money. Here is a fine description of the man,

> 'His appearance, like everything else about him, was deceptive. Six foot tall, big boned, immensely strong, with a tousle of corn coloured hair framing a ruddy countenance, when you first met him your thoughts were of a Viking leaping with a war cry from the bow of a long ship. His voice was high pitched, soft, sometimes hardly audible, the words carefully chosen and precise. … He was a talker, not a chatterer.'

He entered Trinity at sixteen where he read mathematics, which remained an abiding passion all his life. In 1940 he purchased Old Head Hotel at Louisburgh, which he ran with his brother. It was a dilapidated place but he descended upon it with a collection of fifty craftsmen and within three weeks the hotel was ready and three days later opened for visitors.

It was run like a country house. "*I have seen Alec sit down to dinner with two Noble prize winners while at the other tables were a third Nobel winner, the Poet Laureate, and a famous woman historian, Fellows of the Royal Society were two-a-penny,*" remarked one frequent guest.

His knowledge of things was prodigious. He was learned in Elizabethan Mathematics and once set off in a Landrover for Afghanistan. He wished to visit an area where Arab Mathematics met Eastern Chinese Mathematics in pursuit of knowledge in respect of the introduction of zero into mathematics.

He possessed the great gift of friendship and his wife, Betty, his son and daughter, Willy and Lucy, his adopted daughter Mame and many friends mourned his passing.

Old Head, Louisburgh

The road from Mallaranny to Belmullet leads through Ballycroy and Bangor stretching forever across blanket bog and past stacks of hand-cut turf. Small woods of rhododendrons thrive here and load the landscape with rich colour in summer time. Beyond the Srahnamanragh Bridge over the Owenduff the bog expands and stretches to the horizon.

The Parish of Ballycroy stretches from Mallaranny to the south of Bangor Erris and from Nephin Beg range to the sea. Beginning in the Nephin Beg range the Owenduff River gathers many tributaries as it meanders to the sea. In Irish it would translate as the Black River.

The archaeological remains in the area suggest that it has been inhabited for a long time. In Bunmore West are the remains of *Teampall Éanna*, an early church, in Kilburn there is a mount with two pillar stones. One carries a ringed cross and the other has a diamond pattern on its eastern face.

Erris has passed through many owners: Mylesian tribes, Norman barons, the Barrett family and others. After the Ulster Rebellion in the seventeenth century many northern families moved into this area. In fact at the beginning of the nineteenth century their descendants spoke a northern dialect of Irish. They have been described as being a hardy, low-sized, dark featured race, bold, daring, intrepid in danger, not good tempered but hospitable in the extreme.

It was never easy to make a living in this tough and wide landscape and each year the 'Tatie Hokers' made their way to the farms in Ayrshire. They slept in great barns and cow sheds and they moved from one farm to the next. The following verse, by Peter Joyce, recalls the migration.

When I was a youngster, scarcely sixteen years of age.
I became a tatie hooker to earn my first wage.
Sleeping on the bothy straw bed, I wasn't very keen.
But I didn't mind I was a lad of sixteen.

The journey from Mallaranny to Belmullet is unlike any other journey one could make in Mayo.

Ballycroy

John P McHugh

Westport is a popular tourist town, well served by the local railway station which is the last station on the Dublin – Mayo line. If you listen carefully, you will hear water falling over shallow weirs on the Carrowbeg River as it flows through the town towards the sea. Comfortable stone bridges span this river and linden trees grow beside the pathways, which give it a soft, pleasant appearance.

Westport is a planned town, well-proportioned and still possessing architectural integrity. The Marquis of Sligo in the eighteenth century developed it and employed the services of architect James Wyatt to set out the plans. It has a fine octagon with the statue of Saint Patrick placed on top of a high column. One of the hidden and neglected treasures of Westport is the theatre also designed by Wyatt. It is perfect in form and harmonious in execution. The façade is imposing but beyond the façade is a building waiting to be refurbished. In the Catholic Church are fine Stations of the Cross by Herbert McGoldrick and in the Protestant Church are found excellent pieces with art nouveau carvings. As Sean O'Faolain wrote, '*Westport is a town of delightful corners.*'

Thackeray said of Westport,

'*Were such beauties lying upon English shores it would be a world's wonder; perhaps if it were in the Mediterranean or the Baltic, English travellers would flock to it by hundred.*'

The town and the surrounding area still carry this charm and Westport is a convenient centre for touring some of the finest landscapes in the west of Ireland.

Close to the western margin of Clew Bay stands Westport House. This stately Georgian mansion built in the Paladin style was designed by Richard Cassels. It began its architectural life as an east-facing house. After Peter, the second Earl of Altamont married Elizabeth Kelly, who was heiress to a sugar fortune, he enlarged the house by adding three sides to it. The imposing entrance to the house belongs to this era. Within is a splendid main hall and chandeliers and to the left is a fine library with great leather bound tomes. The plasterwork by James Wyatt can be observed in the fine dining room. The house has withstood all the vagaries of history and stands proudly on the edge of Clew Bay.

John P. McHugh

When I was young my parents brought our family to Kilsallagh, which is situated between Murrisk and Louisburgh. This bay was to leave a lasting impression upon me. It is an impression of joy and happiness. The world seemed fresh and young and to this day when I take the southern road along the bay I still feel a lightness of heart. A small road led from Prendergast's house down to an intimate cove. Each morning The Reek greeted me. Its flanks ran with deep harmonious colours. When the sun shone directly upon it, it was light purple. As the sun sank in the west the purple grew darker and the dinted sides carried a darker colour still, deep as blackberry. On the summit of Croagh Patrick stood the small white chapel. On summer days it was sparkling white. There were days also of low mists and clouds but I chiefly remember the sunshine.

At night the beams from the lighthouses probed the darkness with vectors of light. One lighthouse was on an island to the north, the other was on Clare Island. They made me feel secure as I lay in bed. Clew Bay is studded with gentle islands. They are really submerged drumlins and it is said that there are as many islands in the bay as there are days in the year.

Westport was once a busy port as we can gather from the photographs of great masted schooners anchored at Westport Quay. Multi-storied warehouses line the road running beside the quay. Grace O'Malley's fleet once sailed this bay with impunity. Her ships sailed down the coast to France and Spain carrying hides and salted fish to southern ports.

James Cahill is now restoring the coastguard station at Rosmoney. It was built to protect the coast against smugglers and to make sure that maritime law was enforced.

There is no cove or headland along this bay that has not its own folklore, legends and beauty.

Clew Bay

John P. McHugh

Like all monasteries in County Mayo, Murrisk Abbey is situated in a most pleasant place. A path leads directly to Croagh Patrick and some begin their pilgrimage here. The sea laps at its edge.

Father William Bourke's poem written in Irish in 1730 recalls the beauty of the place,

The Friar's Farewell to Murrisk.
My holy vow of obedience
Bids me to remain here
And abandon lovely Murrisk
And the music of the sea.

It is much more beautiful in the original Irish version.

In 1456 Hugh O'Malley, an Augustinian Friar from Banada, Co. Sligo, was granted a Papal Mandate to acquire a license, '*If all was suitable to build a Monastery at Leithear Mursge, in the Diocese of Tuam, on the land given by Thady O'Malley, a Captain of the nation.*' This Augustinian Abbey is built beside the sea where a fresh stream rustles across a pebbled bed. The Friary, known then as Muriske, was dedicated to Saint Patrick, some of whose relics (including, some say, the bones of his charioteer) are buried there.

In 1574 the abbey was suppressed. Like others ousted by a law which could not be enforced, the friars of Murrisk do not seem to have gone very far; a silver chalice, now in Ballintubber, bears the inscription in Latin, '*Pray for the soul of Theobald, Viscount Mayo and his wife Maeve ne Chnochonre, who had me made for the Monastery of Murske in the year of our Lord 1635*' and local folklore has the Friars around a long time after that.

Surviving are the nave-and-chancel church with unusual battlemented walls, fine switch-line tracery in the east window and portions of the east range of the cloister.

Where the pilgrims prepare to climb The Reek, they are reminded of the Great Famine as they study the Famine Ship sculpted by John Behan. It has become a familiar icon. Close to Owen Campbell's comfortable pub is the start of the pilgrim path which takes them on their first steps to the summit.

Murrisk

John P McHugh

This slender castle stands on the seashore of Achill Island. Well proportioned and constructed with authority, it has an eye to the sea and controls the entrance to Achill Sound as the maritime interests of the O'Malleys were in mind when it was built.

The tower at Kildavnet is thought to have been built by Clan O'Malley about 1429 but it is associated locally with Grace O'Malley. Situated at the mouth of Achill Sound it protects the passage that connects Clew Bay with Blacksod Bay.

Castles of this stamp and mould are found all over Ireland. Built both for defence and status, like others, Kildavnet Castle was a fortress which became a manor house.

This typical tower-house was four storeys high with a slight slope at the base. The lower floors were arched over with a stone vault. Entrance was through a doorway leading into a ground floor. There was a "murder hole" through which stones could be thrown at the enemy. Machicolations (an opening between a wall and a parapet) were often set at roof level. The top floor was usually reserved for the owner. Along the walls were arrow slits. The furniture in these buildings was sparse – a table, chairs and benches, a bed with the floor covered with rushes.

Close by is the ancient church and cemetery of Kildavnet. Its foundation date is a matter for debate and it may belong to the early Christian foundations. Close at hand you will find two monuments to two of Achill's greatest tragedies, Kirchintollach 1937 when ten Achill Islanders lost their lives in a 'bothy' (hut) in Scotland, where they were working on the potato harvest and the Clew Bay Drowning of 1894, when thirty-two people from Achill were drowned when a hooker capsized in Clew Bay.

A report reads,

'…at first glance, we were able to see that when the mast struck the water, the mainsail and jib had imprisoned under them several of the poor islanders. The water was a struggling, screaming mass of human beings. Some were grabbing their companions in order to try and save themselves; but the inevitable result was they were dragging one another underneath.'

The bodies were brought as far as Mallaranny by train on the new line that was being built from Westport to Achill Sound. A sad communal grave marks the spot where most of the victims were buried.

Kildavnet Castle

John P. McHugh

The Erriff River does not flow directly into Killary Harbour. It falls over a long waterfall before it finally reaches the sea. It has run sinuously between the Sheeffry Hills and the Partry Mountains, gathering tributaries as it moves along from its source close to Croagh Patrick. During the summer it is quiet, and reduced to a trickle, in winter charged by rain bursts it rushes noisily forward. It forms sand islands along the way and is sometimes doubtful of its course. Then it reaches the waterfall, shreds itself into foam, falls evenly and rushes forward between boulders. Sometimes Ashleigh Falls is quiet, its voice hushed. Sometimes it is thunderous and dramatic.

It has featured in the film of *The Field* by John B. Keane. Taking advantage of its dramatic backdrop the protagonists do final battle here. The scene is made more dramatic by the fact that it takes place at night and against the thunderous sound of falling water.

Michael Viney, writer and journalist, who lives in Thallabawn, on the western side of Mweelrea has written lyrically of this area in his book *A Year's Turning*. With his wife Ethna he has lived in this area for twenty years and celebrated this dramatic landscape in all its moods and at all its levels.

He describes the months of the year as they pass before him and he draws upon memory and reminiscence from his past life. The paragraphs are always tone perfect.

This is how he draws *A Year's Turning* to its conclusion,

'At the winter solstice, the fire goes out beyond Tully Mountain across the bay. Its smouldering afterglow is reflected in the channel as a strip of crimson neon in the cold black sand, and even before it has faded the stars are glittering behind me, over Mweelrea. The silhouette of the mountain cuts off the world to the east, enhancing the private prospect of infinity. Around me in the garden, blackbirds are squealing in the shadows, and a wren, feeling the cold, whirs past in a blur of stubby wings. Yet what I am thinking about, and making a point of it, is O'Connell Street in Dublin, where the wagtails are drifting down to roost above the coloured lights in the plane trees. It is the only time of the year when I feel the least care for the city, such is the potency of Christmas Past.'

Ashleigh Falls

John P. McHugh

Doohooma is a magical place. It is at the end of a broad peninsula and the sea lies about it. Doohooma Head can be treacherous for boats and in 1823 the cutter *Harlequin* was totally wrecked here and all aboard lost. The word itself means The Mound of the Sand Bank.

On summer days the great bundles of cotton cloud pass across the ample skies. Sand and sea and sky and a low-lying landscape give this area a unique charm. The eye always looks to the waves and Achill lying firmly to the south. One falls asleep to the sound of the sea.

The beauty of Doohooma masks a harsher past. The famine was to take a heavy toll on this area and mass burials took place at the lisheen on the sand banks. This lovely landscape has been bleached and blighted by emigration for in the early days it was difficult to wrench a living from the land and the sea. There was no alternative but to join the squads of workers and take the ship anchored off Doohooma Head and sail for Scotland.

Some of these 'tatie hookers' have recorded their experiences. They are never miserable and there is little self-pity in their narratives.

"All the money we earned except for the groceries was sent home every week. Francey, our ganger, would come around every Saturday morning to collect the money to be sent home…we were like a big family, everything was shared. I can honestly say they were hard but happy times."

At the entrance to the peninsula is situated Gweesalia. John M. Synge visited this area and many others and was inspired by remoteness and the folklore of north Mayo. It would find its way into his plays particularly *The Playboy of the Western World*.

Doohooma belongs to Kiltane Parish. This is derived from *Cill Séadhna*, the Church of Séadhna. The name is an old Christian name and there is a very famous story in Irish about a man called Séadhna who fooled the devil.

Every year in August races are held on the strand and each year they become more popular. Recently the Doogort Gold Hoard was discovered close to Gweesalia in a sand bank.

This is a unique maritime peninsula with its eye always towards the sea.

Doohooma

Glenamoy lies between Balderg and Belmullet. The Glenamoy River, which rises east of Glencalry and close to Benmore Mountain and upon which Glenamoy is situated, runs through blanket bog and enters the sea at Sruwaddacon Bay. On this fine river the fisherman can fish for salmon and sea trout and the river has always been a lure to those who wish to escape from the pressures of cities and towns. Fishing and hunting lodges were built in the area "for the quality and by the quality" during the nineteenth century. It is a good river to fish after rain and sea trout run from July until September.

The area has a long archaeological history and it can be read in the blanket bog, which covers the area. A bank of peat carries a history ranging over ten thousand years. Working up through a pollen diagram one discovers dense woodland growing here at one period, and then there is evidence of agriculture and at another level is found Bronze Age activity. Higher up it is evident that agriculture gave way to the treeless landscape which now greets the eye. Charred pine stumps occur close to this area and there is a continued debate as to the cause of this. Was there a natural fire in the area some thousands of years ago or did Bronze Age people clearing the land cause the fires?

During the 'troubles' as we call them, The National army was ambushed by the Irregulars at Glenamoy, losing six men in the battle. As a result, the government introduced internment and the death penalty was introduced for those found with illegal arms.

Life is never easy in an area bereft of good land. But today there is positive growth in the area with the erection of new houses.

The famine and mass emigration broke Celtic culture. In 1851 over three hundred thousand people spoke Irish as their natural language. By 1911 it had withered to seventeen thousand. This is a Gaeltacht area and with the foundation of a new Irish school the language has survived here.

Glenamoy

John P Mc Hugh

Foxford lies on the Moy River. From the bridge one can see the famous Foxford Woollen Mills, which lifted the area out of poverty and misery at the end of the nineteenth century. Foxford blankets became famous all over the world and are still prized for their colour and their comfort.

The story of Foxford Woollen Mills is heroic. The Bishop of Aconry asked Mother Arsenius to improve the conditions of the people. He could not have asked a better person. She got things done and would be considered now as an entrepreneur. She went to County Tyrone and sought advice. She was told by the cognoscenti to go home and say her prayers for they thought that she was undertaking an impossible task. She would not be intimidated and founded the great mills, which were powered by the river, in 1892. They were called the Providence Mills for obvious reason. These mills gave heart and purpose to the town and on the grave of this Kerry woman are inscribed the words,

She hath opened her hand to the needy,
And stretched out her hand to the poor.

The poet F. R. Higgins was born in Foxford in 1896, into a Unionist Protestant family. He resisted pressure from his father to enlist in the First World War. He was an influential presence in his day. His poetry collection includes *Island Blood*, *The Dark Breed*, *Arable Holdings* and the *Gap of Brightness*.

Another famous Foxford native was Admiral William Brown who is known as the 'Father of the Argentine Navy.' He was born in 1777 and immigrated with his family to America at the age of nine. Pressed into the Navy he rose in the ranks and commanded an English merchant vessel against Napoleon. He was imprisoned and eventually escaped to London. He left for Buenos Aires in 1809 where he accepted a command in the Argentinean Navy and defeated the Spanish. He retired, but in 1825, when Brazil declared war against Argentina, he took command of the Navy again. Twice he defeated much larger forces but eventually he was forced to surrender when his ship ran aground. He remained in the service until 1845 and died in 1857. He is proudly remembered in Foxford and is a national hero in Argentina.

The Argentinean sculptor Vergottini executed the bronze bust of this man, which was presented to the town.

John P McHugh

History is often embedded in town names. No more so than Claremorris. It derives its names form Maurice de Prendergast, who arrived in Ireland with Strongbow in 1170 and was later given a large portion of land in South Mayo. The name in Irish is sweeter – *Clár Chloinne Mhuris* – which means the plain of Clann Mhuiris. The name finds it way into the poem of home longing by Raftery, which runs thus,

In the Town of Claremorris I'll spend the first night there
And in Balla that's beyond it I'll sit down and drink.

Although the town itself has existed for about three hundred years there are many ring forts in the area and this extends the history back more than a thousand years.

Ballinasmalla Abbey was founded in 1288 by the Prendergast family and was an expensive building with its own millrace. The infamous Denis Browne came to live at Claremont House after the 1798 Rebellion. He was called *Donncha an Rópa* (Denis of the Rope) because of the manner he dealt with the rebels of 1798. He died in 1828. Raftery the poet has written vicious verses about him.

Geoffrey Browne had his great house built at Castlemagarrett in 1846 shortly after his marriage to Mary, daughter of Daniel Prendergast, the previous owner of the estate. But the old Castlemagarrett, firm, square and resolute was built in the thirteenth century on the banks of the Robe River.

Claremorris enumerates amongst its famous people Sir John Grey, Canon Ulick J. Bourke, Cardinal John Dalton, Connor Maguire and Edward Delaney. Ulick J. Bourke was one of the founders of the Society for the Preservation of the Irish Language, the Gaelic Union, and Irisleabhar na Gaeilge, and he contributed a series to the nation on Easy Lessons or Self-Instruction in Irish.

The canals gave way to the railways and the rapid extension of the railways during the middle of the nineteenth century formed a network all over Ireland. The railway arrived in Claremorris in 1862 and the line from Claremorris to Ballinrobe was one of the last to be built in the nineteenth century. The service lasted sixty-seven years. Owen Malone made the first journey on the train called *The Bat* and Jack Monaghan made the last.

Claremorris

Ballyhaunis lies at the eastern end of the county. It is a thriving community and there is always a sense of optimism about the place. It has a good historical pedigree- with one of the highest concentrations of Megalithic monuments in the west of Ireland. It abounds in ring forts, souterrains, burial mounds, church sites, wedge tombs, crannogs and ancient cooking sites. The discovery of a four thousand year dugout boat at Aughamore confirms the presence of people in this area for a long time.

The Norman family D'Angulo obtained land here in the thirteenth century. After the Tudor conquest Sir Theobald Dillon became the chief landowner. These names are part of the waves of history which have washed over Mayo.

The MacJordans founded an Augustinian Friary here circa 1432 on substantial acreage and it provided well for the people for it was a school and infirmary. A sign of our more religiously diverse times is seen in the establishment of a mosque in Ballyhaunis built by Halal Meat Packers which is, I suppose, the most westerly mosque in Europe.

Two great writers are associated with this town. Fair Cassidy an Augustinian monk who wrote *An Caisideach Bán* and *Máire Bhéal Átha hAmhnais*. Like Saint Augustine he suffered the sting of the flesh and was drawn between monastic life and love for a woman. Douglas Hyde described him as 'The Troubled Friar'.

The other famous writer associated with Ballyhaunis is Bill Naughton. His family moved to Bolton and in 1943 his first story *Ghost Driver* was published. He drove a coal lorry for a living and found that the shaping of a single sentence brought him out in thicker sweat than did loading a few tons of coal. But not deterred he went on to write amongst other works *Alfie*. It was Bill who brought the northern English voice into British Television and *Coronation Street* grew out of his writing. His contribution to English literature has been quite profound. Two of his plays ran simultaneously on Broadway.

His biography ran into four volumes; *On The Pig's Back, Saintly Billy, Neither Use Nor Ornament* and finally *Voices from a Journal*. He died in January 1992 on the Isle of Man. Each year at Aghamore, a summer school is held in his honour and amongst its patrons is his wife Erna Naughton.

Ballyhaunis

John P Mc Hugh

Mayo Abbey is a quiet and remote place set in fertile earth. The abandoned church and the gable of an older church belie the fact that it was once a huge monastic foundation and that scholars came from England to university there.

The origins of the monastery begin at the Synod of Whitby when Saint Colman disagreed with the findings of the council on the date for the celebration of Easter.

He had become a monk at Iona, and so famous were his virtues and learning, as is testified by Bede, that on the death of Saint Finan in 661 he became Bishop of Lindisfarne. The cause he championed was lost at Whitby. He resigned as Bishop of Lindisfarne and left for Iona, carrying some of the relics of Aidan, the first Bishop of Lindisfarne, and some of its treasures with him. His brethren followed him eventually ending up on Inishbofin. Unfortunately there was a dispute between the Irish monks and the Saxon monks. It was for the Saxon monks that Colman founded Mayo Abbey.

This monastery flourished. Its enclosure covered more than twenty-eight acres and Saint Gerald and his monks were endowed with grants of land of over 2,000 acres. Saint Gerald, the son of a northern English King, who had been annoyed at Colman's treatment at Whitby, followed him and was appointed first abbot of Mayo Abbey.

The school gained greatly in fame for sanctity and learning under this youthful abbot. About 679, Adamnan, the biographer of Saint Columba visited Mayo and some believe that he ruled there for seven years after Saint Gerald's death.

By the year 700 AD the monastery had become famous as a seat of learning. Saxon Kings amongst others were educated here. The venerable Bede records the existence of the abbey in the *Ecclesiastical History of the English People*.

Little of its great importance is in evidence as one looks at the site today. But it was in its time famous and respected. A sympathetic archaeological dig could reveal that it was as important as Clonmacnoise. The fact that an ancestor of mine is buried there makes it dear to me.

Mayo Abbey

Mayo, People and Place

The North of Mayo possesses a dramatic landscape. It fronts Sligo Bay with tall-layered cliffs. Beneath, the tortured waves rage against the base of sandstone and limestone layers. The sea is winning the struggle. It claws at substance of rocks and undermines the majestic cliffs. In the end the sea will win.

It is a rugged landscape, with its purple heather and maroon furze bushes. It is sheep and turf country but here and there in the base of the hills is a fertile pocket.

It was not always so: at another time some six thousand years ago the landscape was different. The temperature was warmer, the ecosystem more varied and the land was good. It was the good land which attracted the first Stone Age settlers. How they reached these northwestern shores will always remain a question for debate. Did they arrive in great leather boats with their seeds and their animals? How did they find

their way to the very eastern edge of Europe? There is good evidence that these Stone Age people settled widely in Mayo but we have the best example of their settlement at the Céide fields between Ballycastle and Balderg. The landscape is now boggy and runs to the flank of a large hill. It is difficult to access but it has not always been so, for beneath this sphagnum and turf surface lies the remnants of a pastoral and agricultural civilization.

The archaeologist whose name is most associated with this important agricultural site is Doctor Séamus Caulfield. His father had drawn attention to the fact that when local farmers cut down through the peat they discovered collapsed stone walls and Séamus was to spend a good deal of his archaeological life excavating this blanket bog. Underneath he found the remains of a vast walled system of large pasture fields and he mapped out whole field systems of two to five hectares beneath the bog. Thus was discovered a Stone Age community, highly organised, very efficient and capable of building not only protective walls and wall-based habitations but raising great monuments to its dead. This single discovery was to change archaeological thinking on early European agriculture.

The beginning of the history of Mayo is thus set in stone and land. There is other evidence of these first settlers spread across Mayo but it is most in evidence here. These early settlers, who cleared great forest areas, planted wheat and barley and fished in the rivers and the sea, have left us many Megalithic tombs as a mark and a reminder of their presence. They were a pastoral people with a language, a social system and rich burial ritual.

The Bronze Age became personal to me when I taught at Glenisland National School. A local man named Michael Joyce had discovered a finely crafted sword while swimming in Beltra Lough, which feeds into Clew Bay. Its poise and balance were perfect, its casting clean and exact. Thus whenever I began to teach about the Bronze Age I fetched it from his house.

Such artefacts are important because there is no monumental evidence of the Bronze Age in Mayo as the Bronze Age people had a simple method of burial known as cist burials and pit burials. These are difficult to discover although several have been found in Mayo. No one can give an exact date for the arrival of the first copper or Bronze Age people but a rough date might be 2000 BC. It was a long time ago and there is always uncertainty about exact dates. But we have fine evidence of gold and bronze being worked from the very earliest age. Two delicate sun discs with fine decorations have been discovered at Rappa Castle, near Crossmolina, which belong to this age. Gold too was abundant in Mayo and gold flakes can still be discovered in many of the streams close to Croagh Patrick. It was a culturally active era and the artefacts from the time demonstrate this.

These early settlers were to be supplanted by the Celts who brought with them iron which gave them the edge over the Bronze Age culture. They arrived in the second half of the first millennium although there is no surviving evidence of a large-scale invasion and unfortunately iron rusts. The Turoe Stone, County Galway is the closest evidence we have of them, and from this we assume that they were also present in Mayo.

We are on more certain grounds with the arrival of Saint Patrick. Or are we? His autobiography is interesting from the fact that it lacks all geographical certainty.

In his fine book, *A History of Ulster*, Jonathan Bardon writes,

*' "I, Patrick, a sinner, the simplest of country men…
was taken away into Ireland in captivity with every so
many thousands of people." It is with these words of the
Confession, inscribed in halting Latin and copied into
the Book of Armagh, that written Irish history begins.'*

While Armagh may claim him as their own, there is now
a school of thought which links him firmly with Mayo and
some believe that when he fled from Ireland in a ship it was
from Clew Bay.

Standing above Clew Bay lies the sacred mountain of
Croagh Patrick. Pagan and Christian, it has always been a sacred mountain. Pilgrims have worn a path to the summit and
there is no time of year and no time of day that some pilgrim
is not making his or her way to the top. Patrick, in imita-
tion of Moses, spent forty days upon the summit. If we are
to believe the descriptions in *The Life of Saint Patrick* written
by a north Mayo writer, Tírechán, the Saint did not arrive in
Mayo as a poor priest. He arrived as a bishop, with a massive
retinue and brought with him a household of professionals, a
bishop, a priest, a judge, masons and many others.

We can deduct many things from this list. First, he was a
highly organised man and he meant business. Second, he had
the appearance of man or a chief of some importance who
could have dealt with kings and chieftains as an equal. Third,
he brought with him books and ornaments which would be

imitated. Fourth, he probably kept up a correspondence with
all the monasteries he founded much in the same manner as
Saint Paul wrote to his converts. The speculation is endless.

He knew what he was about. He knew how the system
worked or in modern parlance the mindset of those he had
come to convert. He did not reject older beliefs out of hand
but rather he imposed his beliefs upon them. He incised
crosses on standing stones and he blessed wells and streams,
which had been worshipped by the druids and priests. It was
a bloodless revolution and an example to other missionaries.

This was the beginning of a golden age. All over Mayo you
will find blessed wells dedicated to Saint Patrick and foundations associated with him or the saints who followed. He
founded small Celtic monasteries that were replaced later by
great abbeys. The church of Patrick was a Celtic church as
opposed to a Norman or a Roman church, which came later.
The most ancient of Irish lyrics demonstrate a great love of
learning and of nature. These are poems, which were written
on the edge of manuscripts and have a fresh charm, which are
still seductive.

Many of these monks set up their hermitages on the islands
off Mayo and were excellent sailors and boatmen. The voyage
of Brendan is a testament to this. He was born near Tralee in
Kerry and founded a large monastery at Clonfert and died at
Annaghdown in County Galway. He has been called Brendan

the Navigator. The story of his voyages are famous and it is said that he reached America.

The foundation of Mayo Abbey from which the country derives its name is most interesting. It all began at the Conference of Whitby and the controversy of when precisely Easter should be celebrated. Saint Colman of Lindisfarne wished to celebrate Easter by the Celtic Calendar. He lost the debate and, being a man of hot temper, he left the conference and returned to Lindisfarne. There he dug up the bones of the Irish monks, passed up to Iona and from there went to Inishbofin off the coast of north Galway where he founded a monastery with those who had joined him including Gerald who became first abbot of Mayo Abbey.

There were two nationalities gathered on Inishbofin and they could not get along together as apparently the Irish offended the Angles with their laziness. During the seasons when there was great need for manual labour and when the harvest had to be gathered, the Irish left the other members of the community to do the work whilst they wandered about seeking alms, which they kept to themselves, returning to the monastery in the winter to share the fruits of the labours of the harvests. In response to this friction Saint Colman founded the monastery of Mayo Abbey for the Angles and Saxons and later it became a great university and some of the Saxon Kings of England were educated there.

These were rich spiritual centuries for Mayo and Ireland and we justly call the age 'The Age of Saints and Scholars'. Very little remains of these great settlements. They were built from clay and wattles and the main central church was built of wood. They have long since disappeared and it is only the word 'Kill' in some townland names which indicates that they ever existed. However there is a small island called Duvillaun More to the south of the Mullen peninsula, which gives us some idea of what these enclosures look like. As there were few trees in the area it was more substantially constructed with a stone oratory and about it some stone cells. Here too are incised pillars found on Iniskea North and South, which are amongst the first indications of church art. This would find its final flowering in three great works of art; one in stone, *The West Cross at Monasterboice*; one in metal, *The Ardagh Chalice* and one in vellum, *The Book of Kells*.

The Vikings in their supple long boats made their appearance off the Irish coast in 795. They came as raiders but found the climate and soil suitable to them and settled at the mouth of rivers and set up their towns and trading posts. There is little evidence that they visited Mayo but they did attack Clonmacnoise so they must have known the sea-lanes along the west of Ireland. This brings up the vexed question of the purpose of the round towers. We are served well by round towers for Mayo possesses five of these structures. The most impressive is at Killala but there is also ones at Aghagower, Meelick, Turlough and Balla.

In Irish a round tower is called a *cloictech*, meaning a bell house, or tower. It has been suggested that they were used as places of refuge during Viking raids, however the worst of the Viking raids were over when the old Irish Annals record the first round towers so the question remains open. Perhaps they were used to call the faithful to prayer or perhaps they could have served the purpose of a lighthouse, directing pilgrims to their destination on dark nights. Whatever their purpose, they are as graceful as minarets and campaniles and still stand firmly on the landscape, fine testaments to a monastic age.

The old order began to change. The Vikings had settled into their new seaport homes. They were finally defeated at the Battle of Clontarf which was more than a struggle between Brian Boru and the Vikings. The men of Leinster came in with the Vikings of Dublin and when the battle was finally finished Brian Boru, his son and his grandson were dead. Ireland was in a weakened state and ripe for a takeover by the Normans. They were to arrive in 1169.

Historians still find it difficult to unravel these confusing years but they heralded religious changes in Mayo. New continental diocesan and parochial systems were set up and new continental orders arrived in the county. They brought with them new building skills and these are still obvious in the graceful windows, cloisters and doors they incorporated into these structures. The first to arrive were the Benedictines, followed by the Cistercians, the Augustinians, the Dominicans and Franciscans. The O'Connors built some churches and abbeys; the Normans and their followers would build others.

The O'Connors were generous builders. Rory O'Connor, who became the last High King of Ireland in 1166, was a patron of the church and Cong Abbey was built under his patronage. Much has been added to the Abbey since, but it was one of the earliest foundations and is important for that reason.

Ballintubber is the most famous abbey in Mayo. It has Patrician roots and has survived all the centuries of difficulty and oppression and today is a vibrant spiritual centre.

Moyne is situated on the shore of Killala Bay and should be visited in conjunction with the neighbouring friary of Grosser. Moyne was built under the patronage of the de Burgos and was consecrated in 1462. It is in good condition with its nave, choir, aisle, chapel, sacristy, transepts and cloister garth along with many other Franciscan features.

Mayo then is rich in medieval religious foundations. They were built under the patronage of Irish kings and Norman Lords. The Norman Lords not only built and endowed new abbeys they also built formidable castles for they had come to stay. The chief amongst them in the area was Richard Mór De Burca. Finding cause to dispute with the O'Connors he invaded Connaught in 1235. He claimed for himself the title

'Lord of Connaught.' Marrying Hodierna of the O'Connor Clan, he was an astute politician who set discord amongst the O'Connors (who were now a waning power) and by the time he died in 1243 he had established a strong power base in the province.

His descendants became formidable power players in Ulster politics. Richard Mór's son, Walter, became Earl of Ulster and he skilfully exploited the dynastic rivalries of Gaelic Ulster. His son Richard or the Red Earl ruled with an iron hand and he pushed his territory deep into Inishowen peninsula.

The De Burgo family, whose name takes many forms (Bourke in Mayo and Burke in Galway and De Burca in Irish), had many military allies and these were to form the great Norman families of Mayo. They included the Stauntons, Prendergasts, Fitzgeralds, Butlers and Barry d'Exeters and d'Angulos. They parcelled out the lands of Mayo between them.

Names such as Barrett, Lynnot, Walshe, Joyce and Merrick are associated with the Norman families. Many of these names still form the tissue and web of Mayo life although as time passed many of them changed their names into Irish forms. The elusive d'Angulos became familiarly known as Costello and Waldron. The name d'Exeter is no longer familiar in Mayo but the descendants of these families took on the name Jordan or Mac Siúrtáin and so with all the other great

families. The bloodlines are still there but under more familiar names. They built their castles and settled into the life of Mayo. The finest of these castles was built by Jordan d'Exeter at Ballylahan. It is a formidable structure, set in a strategic position. Like many of the Normans they became more Irish than the Irish themselves.

What, you might ask, happened to the original stock of people who had worked the land, tilled the fields and carried on the daily work. They continued their lives under the Normans. The ancient owners of these lands were expelled to poorer and less extensive lands. The O'Garas, the O'Haras, the O'Dowds and the O'Connors now in reduced circumstances moved to Sligo and Roscommon. Only one old Irish family grimly held out against all these changes and they were the O'Malleys of Clare Island. A formidable clan, they were seafarers and their great leader was Grace O'Malley, the Sea Queen. Her story has been told and retold. Many fine novels have been written about her, including one by Eleanor Fairburn entitled *The White Sea Horse* and another called *Gráinne* by Morgan Llewelyn. Ann Chambers has written an authoritative biography of this formidable woman entitled *Granuaile*.

As the storyteller said '*things rested so*' but the historian knows that things never rest and they have never rested in the story of Mayo. There is always change and movement. The Gaelic Chieftains, prior to the arrival of the Normans, had destroyed their ability to confront an enemy with their internecine wars. Now the descendants of the Norman invaders, the Burkes, began to fight amongst themselves. The Mayo Burkes fought with the Clanrickard Burkes of Galway and with many others. They formed alliances and they broke them. They were always energetic in the pursuit of their goals and the protection of their territories. In 1504 the Mayo Burkes joined with the Lord Deputy Garrett Mór Fitzgerald, The Great Earl of Kildare against Clanrickard. It is an era stained with blood.

However elsewhere in the known world events were occurring which would have a lasting impact on life in Mayo. In England, Henry VIII, a Catholic was raised to the throne in 1509. On October 31st, 1517, Martin Luther nailed his 95 theses on the door of the castle church at Wittenberg. This marked the beginning of the Reformation. In 1521, Henry had written a thesis against Martin Luther for which he received high praise from the Pope and the title of Defender of the Faith and this motto is still franked on English coins. He came into conflict with the Pope over affairs of the heart and the English Reformation came into being. Between 1536 and 1540 all the monasteries in England were dissolved and their property confiscated. An oath of supremacy to Henry was required from all his subjects. In 1541, some years before his death, Henry declared himself King of Ireland.

This had little immediate impact but with the ascent of Elizabeth to the throne in England, things began to change. The government in Dublin had been trying to impose some type of order on the disorder in Connaught. The Lord Deputy, Sir Henry Sidney procured submission from the warring De Burgos and Sir Edward Fitton was appointed President of Connaught. His task was to set out the borders of the new counties of Connaught but this drew the Burkes into rebellion. This was followed by several other short-lived outbreaks of war. It was the new Lord Deputy, Sir John Perrott, who finally established the boundaries of Mayo under the general title '*The Composition of Connaught*'.

The nature of land possession changed. The title of chieftain was abolished and land possession was firmly established with the introduction of a system of primogeniture. This brought with it a certainty, which had not existed before, and the clan system drew to an end. But the Burkes again rebelled and were suppressed by the new Governor of Connaught, Sir Richard Bingham. Bingham (1528-1599) was a tough career soldier. He lived through tempestuous times and saw action as a sea captain. He was sent to Ireland by Elizabeth to help suppress the Desmond Rebellion and he took part in the massacre of Spanish and Italian soldiers at Smerwich, Co. Kerry. He governed with a tough hand and was ardent in the use of the death penalty. It is said that he put to death a thousand survivors of the Spanish Armada.

The Spanish Armada was a great fleet assembled in 1588 to invade England but was dogged by failure from the beginning. Defeated by the British, the fleet sailed around Scotland and the west of Ireland. In stormy weather twenty-three ships were wrecked on the Irish coast. Sir William Fitzgerald, Lord Deputy of Ireland, a quarrelsome and corrupt man, gave orders to execute Spaniards when they came ashore. Over six thousand were drowned, killed or captured. Bingham claimed that he put 1100 to death.

"Thus," he wrote, *"having made a clean dispatch of them we rested Sunday all day, giving thanks to Almighty God for Her Majesty's most happy success and deliverance from her most dangerous enemies."*

Sir George Carew wrote,

"The miseries which they sustained on this coast are to be pitied in any but the Spaniards. Of those who came to the land by swimming or enforced thereto by famine, near 3000 were slain."

And the Irish were not beyond blame in the matter. Bingham had ordered all who came ashore alive were to be brought to him but the Irish had no interest in obeying his orders. Dead men tell no tales and many were murdered for their velvet coats and golden chains. It is said that Owen O'Malley killed the crew which landed on Clare Island and there is the story of Melaghlen McCabb whose encounter with the Spannish was described thus,

"They were so miserably distressed coming to land that one man named Melaghlen McCabb killed eighty with his gallowglass axe."

Much of Mayo history relates to the sea and one of its most remarkable figures was Grace O'Malley. Born around 1530 into a seafaring family, she is a legendry pirate queen who was married twice and had three children. She changed her allegiance as it suited her. In 1576 she offered the Lord Deputy, Sir Henry Sidney, the use of her galleys and two hundred men but later she came into conflict with English forces in Connaught and spent time in Dublin Castle. In 1593 she sailed to London where she met Queen Elizabeth and secured property rights for her children. Like Sir Richard Bingham she lived through tempestuous times and possessed a tempestuous character. She knew how the political winds were blowing. Her son, called Tibbot na Long, is said to have been born on board ship, during one of her western raids. He was later to become the first Viscount of Mayo. The political winds had changed. The eldest son now held the ownership of land and the old system of succession was changed forever. We do not know where she is buried. Many believe that she rests in the O'Malley tomb in the Carmelite friary on Clare Island. Almost everywhere around Clew Bay is associated with her memory. Her presence still haunts its shores and islands.

Grace's son Tibbot na Long together with the Governor of Connaught sided with Mountjoy against O'Neill at the battle of Kinsale and this stood much in his favour. He became the first Viscount Mayo as a result of this allegiance. He was murdered two years later and his tomb is to be found in the sacristy of Ballintubber Abbey. An imposing Jacobean style tomb marks the spot. The English style of the tomb marks the beginning of a new British system of rule and manners.

In 1609 Ulster was planted with new settlers and there were new arrivals in Mayo. The most prominent were John Browne of the Neale, ancestor of the Marquis of Sligo and of Lord Kilmaine, John Moore and Theobald Dillon who became Viscount Mayo. Thomas Wentworth, later Lord Strafford, considered planting Connaught in the same way in 1635 but it never came to fruition. He died on the scaffold in 1641 abandoned by (and shortly to be followed by) Charles I in whom he had placed his trust. From the documents he drew up for this plantation we know that ten percent of the lands of Mayo were possessed by about a dozen Protestant landowners. The rest was in the hands of about a thousand Catholic landowners.

In 1649 Cromwell arrived in Ireland. His campaign was short and fierce and his name once sent a chill down the spine. The aftershock would reach Mayo in 1653 when his soldiers plundered there. Tirawley was reserved for Cromwellian settlers and the lands of both Lord Mayo and Lord Dillon were confiscated.

When Charles II returned and Cromwell's bones were dragged behind a horse through London it was thought that those who had been faithful to the cause of Charles would have their lands restored. The lands of Lord Mayo and Lord Dillon were restored but others were not so lucky. Many Cromwellian settlers retained their lands. At the close of Charles II's reign the Catholic ownership of land had fallen to forty three percent. Come the Williamite wars and this possession fell to thirty nine percent. Thousands of Irishmen who gained employment with the Catholic armies of Europe were known as the Wild Geese and they fled to the continent and their lands were disposed of. The dark penal laws were introduced and a great number of Catholic landowners became members of the Established Church. As Davitt was to say later "*Land is the first love.*" This was never truer than in Mayo.

With the imposition of the penal laws which started well before 1691, we enter what I have always called The Dark Century. From the beginning of the English Reformation, laws establishing a particular religion and punishing those who did not conform were passed in England and in Ireland. In addition to laws against Catholics, there were statutes relating to Jews, Protestant Dissenters (non-Anglicans), and Quakers. They were harsh beyond all measure on Catholics and intended to destroy the very soul of a people. Among other things they were forbidden to purchase or lease land, forbidden to keep arms, could not attend worship and they could not send their children abroad to receive education. This was an age without a voice. It is heard in sad Gaelic poetry and it is the voice of hidden Ireland and the dispossessed.

Rebellion ripens quietly in such circumstances and it must be said that these laws were not always stringently applied. The testament we have to these dark times in Mayo is in the Mass Rocks which are still pointed out in remote places and in the penal crosses which sometimes turn up. These spare crosses carved often in bog oak have a primitive quality, which is haunting when one considers the dark times in which they were carved.

These became personal to me when a friend of mine, Eddie Cannon, who owned a pub in Castlebar and was a well-read man, showed me one of these sad crosses. To study its stark realism, its spare execution, its lonely crucified figure is to bring reality to a dark century.

But the religious life in Hidden Mayo continued. People went on pilgrimage to Croagh Patrick or visited the holy wells. These holy wells, churches and graveyards were visited on pattern days. Old traditions continued and it must be remembered that the spoken language was that of Irish. The old pagan wakes, with the keening women and at which people danced and sang, smoked their pipes and told stories were vehicles for the transmission of an ancient culture. For an outsider, like William Young or Thackeray, they seemed barbaric. It was a world which lacked elegance. It was the Hidden Ireland but it did have its own cohesion.

Quietly young seminarians slipped out through the western ports and set off to the continent to prepare for the priesthood in many of the Irish colleges spread across the continent. They were to return to Ireland and Mayo as priests or spoiled priests and many of them would carry with them the revolutionary views rife at the time, particularly in Paris.

During these times the small farmer, despite new ownership and new lords, continued to work the land. Many of them were subsistent farmers. The leases to these small patches of land were short and dependant upon the landlords and life was both tenuous and tough. Agriculture became tenuous and many had to migrate each year to work in the farms of Scotland and the north of England. This annual migration lasted into the second half of the last century. But mass emigration had not yet begun. In Achill transhumance took place, when farmers brought their cattle to higher ground in order to pasture there following an ancient practice practised right across northern Europe. Edmund Spencer, the author of

The Faerie Queen, mentions the practice as 'Booleying' and it is also mentioned in the Brehon Law.

The small farmer had held on to his land during the years of change but they served the large estates and the landlords: the hidden Mayo serving the official Mayo.

The towns and villages were well established by now. Some such as Cong, Balla, Ballinrobe, Mayo Abbey, Aghagower and Ballintubber grew up around ecclesiastical centres while others like Ballina, Killala and Westport grew up because of their situation by the sea.

One of Lord Lucan's forefathers, John Bingham founded the town of Castlebar in the early seventeenth century. The town was granted a charter and James I granted it a borough charter in 1611. It became the administrative centre of Mayo. Amongst its claim to fame is the famous incident during the last invasion of Ireland when the French General Humbert routed the English troops who fled to Hollymount and Tuam. The incident became known as 'The Races of Castlebar.'

The story has been well and minutely told in the massive and detailed novel by Tom Flanagan called *The Year of the French*. The French were not supposed to land in Mayo at all, but on the 22nd August 1798 a force under General Jean Joseph Amable Humbert landed at Kilcummen to the north of Killala. It seemed to be an impossible task and an expedition doomed to failure from the very beginning. However, Humbert was a guerrilla fighter and a Napoleonic General. He had no intention of confronting the English forces directly and he did not approach Castlebar along the main route to the town. Instead he force-marched his troops along a rough track along the east shore of Lough Conn and on a night of heavy rain and lightning led his forces and the Irish insurgents through the Windy Gap north of Castlebar.

As they descended upon Castlebar, Humbert drove a herd of cattle in front of his army and his men formed a single lateral line so that cannon fire from the enemy could do little damage. Close to the town he divided his small force so some approached from the south. In the confusion that followed, the British believed that two armies had arrived from France. They abandoned the town and fled as quickly as they could in the direction of Galway. It was a total rout and Humbert declared that Connaught was a republic and John Moore of Moore Hall was declared President.

Humbert for some unexplained reason dallied in Castlebar instead of pursuing his advantage. Many reasons have been given for this, including the reason that he was pursuing an affair with a lady from one of the great houses. The taking of Castlebar and establishing a President of the short-lived new republic were the highlights of the campaign. Far too late he began the push out of Castlebar and he was defeated by General Lake at Ballinamuck. General Humbert and his French troops were treated well and were taken by barge to Dublin.

It is a story with a fair ending for the French but the three thousand Irish recruits who had joined with them – mostly small farmers and the dispossessed belonging to the Hidden Mayo whose voice we hear little of during what I call the Dark Century – did not fare so well. Harried as they retreated, they were massacred and an Irish text described how the pigs fattened on their bodies.

There was a flourishing linen industry in Mayo during the Napoleonic war and, by the early nineteenth century, all over the county the spinning wheels were busy. After the Battle of the Diamond in 1795 more than four thousand refugees from Ulster arrived in Mayo and some of these were weavers. Two hundred looms were in use in Castlebar and the product was sold in the Linen Hall. Linen Hall Street is a testament to the industry of these weavers but by the mid 1830s the industry was failing. A monument in bronze called The Linen Stream at a roundabout in Castlebar celebrates these vanished industries. Great mill houses were set up on the banks of streams and the water channelled to drive the great millwheels. But many have been knocked down and others are bleak and empty husks.

In Achill, Rev. Edward Nangle set up his mission in 1831. He was a controversial but energetic figure and he did set up his colony on a bleak landscape. The story of this missionary endeavour and his proselytising methods are well told in Teresa McDonald's book *Achill Island*. In the book a photograph of the colony, well-ordered against a rough mountain landscape is a testament to his determination and drive.

In Galway, the Mayo born poet Anthony Raftery who was to die in 1835 was writing in Irish. He was born in Killedan. His father possessed a small insignificant parcel of land. He was born blind and later in life he was banished from Killedan because he had destroyed a fine horse belonging to Frank Taffy his employer. He spent the rest of his life wandering in south Galway, playing music badly and writing poetry. Much of it was on contemporary issues such as *The Galway Elections*, *The Whiteboys* and many others. But he is best remembered for his poem, *County Mayo*, one of the most popular poems ever written in Irish. He died in 1835 on the eve of Christmas morning. In 1900 Lady Gregory at her own cost set a tombstone above his grave in Kleenex cemetery.

Riocard Bairéad from Belmullet was also a fine Gaelic poet and took part in the rebellion of 1798. His poem *Preab san Ól* is a rollicking drinking song and his poem *Eoghan Coir* is a blistering satire on a local bailiff. The great poet Thomas Cassidy, the Augustinian friar, from Ballyhaunis died in

1775. He possessed a troubled mind, his heart torn between the flesh and the spirit.

Harp music was very popular in Mayo. Carolan was a visitor to the great houses and wrote music to celebrate their owners. The Mayo harpists Charles Fanning and Hugh Higgins continued his tradition. And during these dark and difficult times the old culture was passed on through oral tradition. The value of these traditions would be later recognised by Yeats and Lady Gregory. The man who would save a dying language and help restore it was the first president of Ireland, Douglas Hyde. His service to the culture of this country is inestimable.

But in Mayo, as in all Ireland, the nineteenth century was to be marked by The Great Famine, the Land War and the Land Reforms, which were to change the face of the county and the ownership of the land. Two names would emerge from this century, Michael Davitt, the patriot and Captain Boycott who could give a new word to the English Language.

My father, Darby Mullen, told me stories concerning Michael Davitt. My grandfather, Shoemaker Carney, who lived on the side of a mountain overlooking the lakes, plains and mountains of Mayo and would have known people who were born during the Great Famine. Through these two men the history of Mayo during the nineteenth century became very real to me and I subsequntly wrote two books on the subject of the Great Famine. One was a novel entitled *The Hungry Land* the other was a factual account of the Famine taken from the local newspapers, particularly the *Connaught Telegraph* in whose archive can be found a weekly account of what happened in Mayo during the Darkest Years.

The famine was a tragedy waiting to happen. Fifty years prior to the disaster the population was increasing at a rapid rate and marginal land was brought into use on the sides of rough hills and mountains to produce a single vegetable, the potato, to sustain them. If that failed then the population would be faced with disaster.

The Great Famine, coming as it did, at the middle of the nineteenth century was a great divider. When it was finished the small cottiers and the marginalized were wiped out. The culture of Hidden Mayo was almost destroyed, a great number of people had died, emigration became endemic, the high mountain fields were abandoned and returned to rough grass and the Mayo voice became sad. The great famine left a scar upon our memories and sapped our energy.

There had been famines before but the Great Famine between 1845 and 1850 was the deepest and the worst of all. The blight, which affected the potatoes, became apparent in 1845 but in 1846 there was a second failure and 1847 became known as Black 47. Here are some short accounts taken from the *Connaught Telegraph* and penned by the editor Lord Cavendish,

> *"You had a jubilee* [he is speaking of the merchants] *for the last eighteen months, while those wretched creatures, scarce able to move, were seen crawling forth, carrying the dead bodies of husband and wife and child, without coffin for internment. While you were amassing riches how many of your countrymen were buried in their own cabbage plots or whole families interred in their own cabins by tumbling their roof in on them."*

Many of these merchants were Catholics and many Catholic farmers exported much of their grain and animals. A final quotation from that fatal year,

> *"In '46 people were killed in hundreds. In '47 they were mowed down in thousands. In '46 they got Christian sepulchre but in '47 they were thrown into holes dug in cabbage gardens, in fields without coffins. And we have seen the dead carried about in the arms of females begging from door to door."*

Not only did the poor and the weak die of hunger but famine fever struck. This added to the dreadful tragedy. There was little escape from this visitation. Some fled to the workhouse. The workhouses could not cope with the numbers and in Castlebar people died outside the gates. Many headed for the ports to escape the malignant fever. The famine ridges on high famine fields remain to this day as sad monuments to these terrible events.

During the years leading up to the famine there were secret societies forming. Chief amongst them were the Ribbonmen who were strong in the linen triangle in south central Ulster and in parts of Connaught. Interest was also centred on Daniel O'Connell (the Great Liberator, who campaigned and won Catholic Emancipation and tried to get the Act of Union repealed). On his visit to Castlebar men who had unyoked his horses drew his carriage into the town of Castlebar. There were great celebrations in the town on his arrival. He was to die abroad in 1847 when the famine was most virulent.

Michael Davitt was born during these terrible times in 1846 in Straide. He was to become an agrarian radical, a journalist, and 'Father of the Land League.' He became a friend of Tolstoy and many world leaders and is perhaps one of the greatest to emerge from Mayo.

His father was evicted for non-payment of rent in 1851 and the family migrated to Haslingden, Lancashire. At the age of ten Michael began to work at a cotton mill but when he lost his right arm while working there he took up work as a newsboy and a printer's devil. At the age of sixteen he took evening classes at the Mechanics' Institute and studied Irish history. The desire for knowledge and education never left him and he became proficient in several languages.

He became involved with the Fenians, a revolutionary society founded in 1858 to overthrow British rule in Ireland. The movement became active after the famine and was the most important revolutionary movement in Ireland in the nineteenth century.

For his membership of the Fenians he was sentenced to fifteen years' penal servitude. First he was imprisoned in Millbank and suffered terrible deprivation. He was six feet in stature on entering Millbank; when he left for Dartmoor, ten months later, he measured five feet ten and a half inches. The food at Dartmoor was repulsive and Davitt with his one arm was put to the severest labour. He broke stones, was harnessed to a cart and in summer time crushed bones beside a cesspool. He suffered through all this in silence. He was released after seven years on ticket of leave. He first returned to Mayo where he received a hero's welcome, later leaving for America to join his family who had emigrated.

While in America he met many Fenians, including John Devoy. On his return to Ireland he had two objectives: Home Rule and Land reform. Aided by James Daly he founded The Mayo Land League in 1879. With this movement, chiefly peaceful, he persuaded Charles Stewart Parnell to join him and, at an historic meeting in Westport, Parnell ut-

tered the historic words, "*Hold a firm grip of your homesteads and lands.*" Parnell became president of the National Land League. A land war followed which was chiefly run on passive resistance lines. Their methods were best summarised by Parnell who uttered these words at Ennis,

> "*What are you going to do to a tenant who bids for land from which a neighbour has been evicted? Kill him? No, you must shun him on the roadside, when you meet him, you must shun him in the streets of the town, you must shun him at the shop counter, you must shun him in the fair and in the market place and even in the house of worship.*"

The Land Acts which followed gave the tenants the three Fs – fair rent, fixity of tenure and free sale. The Land League fought for tenant ownership and, with that achieved, the land finally came into the possession of the farmer. It was a magnificent achievement and passive resistance became a weapon against tyrants and governments throughout the world as in India when Ghandi applied the same methods. It also meant the end of landlordism in Ireland. The landlords passed out of existence and their names no longer register as names of importance.

But Davitt had many other interests. He became bankrupt after a County Meath election but later was elected for South Mayo. He spent four years in parliament but it was not to his taste. He was to earn his living from his writings. Among his writings were *Leaves from a Prison Diary*, *The Boer Fight for Freedom*, *The Fall of Feudalism in Ireland* and a book on Russian anti-Semitism.

He died in Dublin on the 30th May 1906 and he is buried in Straide. Here are the following lines from his will,

"To my friends I leave kind thoughts; to my enemies the fullest forgiveness; and to Ireland the undying prayer for the absolute freedom and independence which it was my life's ambition to try and obtain for her."

He is, I believe, the greatest Mayo person in our long and sad history.

If the words 'passive resistance' became popular in political usage another word came into the language during the land wars and that was the word boycott. Captain Charles Cunningham Boycott was born in Norfolk in England. He was a man without any humour. Lacking imagination, he found himself in the wrong place at the wrong time. To begin with he leased land in Achill and tried to bring bad land into production. He was a severe and exacting character and he was hard on his workers, sweating the last penny of wages from them. He remained here for twenty years and then departed for Ballinrobe where he became an agent for Lord Erne.

He was a man of British rectitude and could not accommodate himself to the mindset of the Irish tenants who worked the land. As in Achill he set down several laws; no gates should be left open, no hens on his property, nobody could be late for work and no tenant could collect wood from his estate. One morning a notice was pinned to his gates. He was warned not to collect rents unless they were reduced by a quarter. He evicted three tenants. Backed by the Land League the tenants refused to work for him. He found that he had nobody to feed his cattle, milk the cows or attend to any of the farm duties. He published the situation in *The Times* and some fifty Orangemen, chiefly from Cavan came to assist him. They were followed by troops and the story became world news.

James Daly of the *Connaught Telegraph* was hugely active during this tempestuous time and wrote extensively on the matter. The harvesting of Boycott's crops was a financial disaster and, as Parnell remarked, every turnip dug cost a shilling. Boycott was eventually defeated and he returned to England with his wife and family until the trouble blew over. He had contributed a new word to the English Language.

With the end of the land wars a new ownership of the land had been established. George Moore of Moore Hall celebrated the departure of the landowners. George was a writer of impeccable style and the author of one of the finest autobiographies ever written, *Hail and Farewell*. His influence on

James Joyce through his short stories and *Confessions of a Young Man* was considerable. He brought the realism of the French novel to the English reading public when he wrote *Ester Waters* and his writing on the French Impressionists introduced them to London. He knew them all in Paris, chatted with them familiarly and had his portrait painted by Manet. In fact he painted his portrait three times. He was also familiar with Degas, Pissarro, Renoir and Zola. His novel *The Lake* has made beautiful Lough Carra one of the most celebrated literary lakes in the world.

The life of the great houses lives on in his golden prose,

"I dare not order the trees to be felled at Moore Hall… everything came out of Moore Hall: if Moore Hall had not existed, I should not have existed, not as I know myself to-day, for it was Moore Hall that enabled me to go to Paris, and to sit in the Nouvelle Athenes with Manet and Degas; to gather a literary atmosphere from Hugo, Zola, Goncourt, Banville, Mendes and Cabaner."

If there is a monument to the landed gentry of Connaught and Mayo it is to be found in the works of George Moore.

But if these are the great historical peaks of the nineteenth century there are other events which have shaped our history.

Thursday 21st August 1879 was no ordinary day for the people of Knock. That evening it was raining. Mary McLoughlin and Mary Byrne noticed a great light illuminating the southern gable of the church. Three moving figures appeared before them. They called their neighbours and, gathering in front of the apparition, they recognised the figures of Mary, the Virgin mother, Saint Joseph and Saint John. Although it was raining the ground beneath the gable was dry. What these people witnessed is what, in Mayo, we call The Apparition at Knock. John McHale of Tuam set up a commission to examine the witnesses. They were found trustworthy. They investigated all natural explanations including the magic lantern theory but they could come up with no rational explanation for the event.

Soon pilgrims were flocking to the area and to this day they continue to arrive from all parts of the world. The facilities at Knock have improved during the years and particularly since the energetic Monsignor Horan was placed in charge of the parish. A great cathedral was built under the direction of Archbishop Cunnane and Monsignor Horan built an international airport on the back of a barren hill. Today those immigrants who left Ireland during the fifties, sixties and seventies can fly home from England in less that an hour.

Archbishop McHale was a towering figure during the nineteenth century. He was called "*The Lion of the Fold of Judah,*" and was a formidable figure on the political and religious landscape. He was a child when he saw Humbert and his French-speaking soldiers pass through Lahardaun on the way to Castlebar. His first language was Irish and he was one of its great defenders. He was later to translate the *Iliad* into Irish. He was educated at Maynooth and became Professor of Theology there. He began to write a series of letters in 1820 attacking the tithe system, which obliged Catholics and Non-Conformists to contribute to the Church of Ireland, and appealed for Catholic emancipation and the repeal of the Union. He held uncompromising nationalistic views and was against educating Catholic and Protestant children in the same schools. He objected to the selection of Newman as the first rector of Dublin University. He was inflexible and not tempered by prudence and these faults led to a stormy career. When he attended the Vatican Council, in 1861, he spoke and voted against Papal Infallibility. It was during his spiritual watch that many of the present-day Gothic-styled churches were built.

Archbishop McHale was at the centre of all the intellectual and political tempests of his day. He lived until he was ninety and is buried in the cathedral in Tuam.

And quietly in the 1860s the railway system, like a blood vein, was stretching into Mayo. The stations would become our wailing walls and my own forebears set off from Manulla Junction for America and England.

On the sporting front the Gaelic Athletic Association was established in 1884 and the Mayo County board established in 1888. Local football clubs were to grow and to flourish and, in 1936 and in 1950, Mayo won two All Ireland football finals. Recently the Mayo Ladies football teams have distinguished themselves by winning several All Ireland finals.

Handball has always been a popular game although it was more popular in the thirties and forties than it is now as the many ruined handball alleys in lonely places testify.

Today, alongside the Gaelic games, tennis, boxing and rugby football flourish in Mayo as does soccer which has been long established here. British sailors and soldiers introduced it in the early 1800s and the last few years, particularly when the famous 'Ban' was removed, it has flourished. Television has made it more popular still.

The twentieth century has seen the changing of the political guard, and has not been without is tribulations and turmoil in Mayo. Land Acts like the Ashbourne were introduced in favour of the farmers and in the first decade of the century several secondary schools and colleges were established. We have come a long way since Archbishop John McHale attended a hedge school in Lahardaun.

1912–14 was to bring a Home Rule Crisis and in 1913 there were riots in Westport after the staging of *General John*

Regan by George Birmingham, who was rector at Westport, because he offended national sensitivities. He was a great lover of Irish literature and counted Horace Plunkett, Arthur Griffith and Douglas Hyde amongst his friends.

The Ulster Crisis brought about the formation of the Irish Volunteers. The first Inspector General of the Irish Volunteers was Colonel Maurice Moore, the brother of George Moore the novelist. He was later to side with John Redmond. The Rebellion of 1916 was to change everything utterly. John McBride, who was married to Maud Gonne, was executed in Dublin for his part in the rebellion. He was born in Westport and this execution swung sympathy towards the Rising although it was initially condemned in the local paper. For a brief historical moment De Valera entered Mayo politics. Both he and his wife Sinéad had come to Toormakeady early in the century to learn Irish in this Irish speaking area and later he would be elected in East Mayo. A time of turbulence followed for a number of years with the War of Independence, the Anglo Irish Treaty and, finally, the divisive Civil War, which was a war which would divide the county politically.

The fighting in Mayo was of short duration, and the fighting was not particularly fierce. The names most associated with this war are Tom Maguire and Michael Kilroy. The capture of Michael Kilroy effectively ended the war in Mayo and the county was fortunate to escape the savage phase which followed when brother fought with brother in other counties. The classic image of these years is represented in the photograph taken by J. J. Leonard of Milroy's flying brigade. The best account we have of these stirring times will be found in Ernie O Malley's autobiographical books *On Another Man's Wounds* and *The Singing Flame*.

The county was now at rest but harsh times were to follow. Secondary and vocational schools continued to be built for education was a priority in Mayo. The economic war lay heavily on the backs of the small farmers. Farmers stood in the markets and barely a beast was sold all day. It was a long, tough economic war lasting some six years. But as always the small farmer came through. He reared his family. Some had to take the boat to England, some could go to the new secondary schools and one would stay on the land.

Emigration continued from Mayo and the hard earned money of the emigrants helped sustain people at home. The stations of Mayo were crowded with emigrants waiting for the train to take them into exile. In the fifties half a million people left the country. They were unskilled, unprepared and unconsidered. Kilburn and Cricklewood became another Irish county. It is a story of bitter exile and Catherine Dunne in her book *An Unconsidered People* gives an account of these times through her interviews with those in England who remember them. They are the lost members of the race. Many did well; some did exceedingly well. Others fell through the net and now live in neglect and poverty.

A younger generation better educated, knowledgeable in the ways of the world and not carrying the heavy burden of history, have emigrated to Britain and Europe. Mayo is part of Europe now. In Mayo we have Knock airport. Every day of the week people take flights to various parts of Europe and the holiday spots on the Canary Islands. Central London is an hour away, the centre of Europe too. Mayo people are no longer forced into exile, they go there by choice. There is employment at home, a sense of optimism, and a sense that we are now our own masters and can bend our own destiny to our own desires.

And every day, during the summer season, tourists visit the Céide Fields and consider how the history of Mayo first began when people from the sea drew up their leather boats, developed the land and set up boundaries around their fields. The history of Mayo was six thousand years in the making.

Acknowledgements

To my wife Deirdre.

To the staff of the Mayo Library, who were more than generous with their time and sources, particularly Ivor Hamrock.
To Donal Downes who drew me away from the task and
to Jane Crosbie who drew me back to the task. To Michael,
John and Ann Carney who are devoted to their Mayo roots.
To Mayo historians, who in articles, journals, newspapers and
periodicals set down the history of the county.

Michael Mullen

Bibliography

Boylan, Henry, *A Dictionary of Irish Biography*, Gill and Macmillan, Dublin, 1975

Byrne and McMahon, *Faces of the West Of Ireland*. The Appletree Press. 1977.

Burke, Éamonn, Burke, Burke and De Burgh, *People and Places*. Dublin, 1995

Chambers, Anne, Granuaile, *The Life and Times of Grace O Malley*. Wolfhound Press, Dublin, 1979

De h-Ide, Dubhglas, *Abhráin agus Dánta and Reachtabhraigh*. Dublin 1933.

Flanagan, Thomas, *The Year of the French*, Macmillan, London 1979.

Hayward. R., *The Corrib Country*. Dundalk. 1943/ 1968.

Hone, Joseph, *The Moores of Moore Hall*. Jonathan Cape, London 1939

Maxwell, W.H., *Wild Sports of the West*. Phoenix Publishing Company. Dublin, 1832.

Killanin and Duignan, *The Shell Guide to Ireland*, Ebury Press. London. 1967.

Knight, P., *Erris in the Irish Highlands and the Atlantic Railway*. 1836.

Lalor, Brian, Editor. *The Encyclopaedia of Ireland*. Gill and McMillan. 2003.

Meehan, Rosa, *The Story of Mayo*. Mayo County Council. 2003.

Miles, George, *The Bishops of Lindisfarne*, Hexham, Chester-le-Street, and Durham. Wells Gardner, Darton. 1898.

Moore, George Augustus, *The Lake, The Untilled Field, Hail and Farewell*, Edited by Richard Allen Cave. Colin Smythe

Mullen, Michael, *The Hungry Land*. Bantam Press. 1986.

Ní Cheanainn, Áine, *The Heritage of Mayo*. Western People, Ballina, 1982.

Ó Caiside, Tomás, *An Caisideach Bán; The Songs and Adventures of Tomás Ó Caiside*, translated from Irish by Adrian Kenny, Greensprint, Ballyhaunis, 1993.

O'Hara, Bernard (ed) *Mayo; Aspects of its Heritage, The Archaeological, Historical and Folklore Society*, Regional Technical College, Galway, Ireland.

O'Malley, Ernie, *On Another Man's Wound*. Anvil Books, Dublin, 1936.

Praeger, Robert Lloyd, with an introduction by Michael Viney, The Collins Press, Cork 1997.

Pochin, Mould, D.C. *The Irish Saints. Claymore and Reynolds.* Dublin. 1964.

Quinn, J.F., History of Mayo –five volumes- Brendan Quinn – 1993-2002.

Reilly, Terry, *Dear Old Ballina.* The Western People, Ballina, 1993.

Somerville-Large, Peter, *The Irish Country House.* Sinclair-Stevenson. 1995.

Welch, Robert, *The Oxford Companion to Irish Literature.* Clarendon Press. 1996.

Thackeray, William M., *The Irish Sketch Book*; Chapman and Hall, London, 1843.

Viney, Michael, *A Year's Turning.* The Blackstaff Press. Belfast 1996.

Waldron, Jarlath, *Maamtrasna. The Murders.* Burke. Blackrock. Dublin.

Wilde, Sir William, *Lough Corrib and Lough Mask.* 1849.

Woodham-Smith, *The Great Hunger.* Old Town Books. New York. 1962

Dear Reader

This book is from our much complimented illustrated book series which includes:-

Belfast	Drogheda & the Boyne Valley
By the Lough's North Shore	Blanchardstown, Castleknock and the Park
East Belfast	Dundrum, Stillorgan & Rathfarnham
South Belfast	Blackrock, Dún Laoghaire & Dalkey
Antrim, Town & Country	Bray and North Wicklow
Inishowen	Limerick's Glory
Donegal Highlands	Galway on the Bay
Donegal, South of the Gap	Connemara
Donegal Islands	The Book of Clare
Sligo	Armagh
Mayo	Ring of Gullion
Fermanagh	Carlingford Lough
Omagh	The Mournes
Cookstown	Heart of Down
Dundalk & North Louth	Strangford Shores

For the more athletically minded our illustrated walking book series includes:-

Bernard Davey's Mourne   Tony McAuley's Glens
Bernard Davey's Mourne Part 2

And from our Music series:-

Colum Sands, Between the Earth and the Sky

We can also supply prints, individually signed by the artist, of the paintings featured in the above titles as well as many other areas of Ireland.

For details on these superb publications and to view samples of the paintings they contain, you can visit our web site at **www.cottage-publications.com** or alternatively you can contact us as follows:-

Telephone: +44 (028) 9188 8033   Fax: +44 (028) 9188 8063

Cottage

Publications

**Cottage Publications
is an imprint of
Laurel Cottage Ltd
15 Ballyhay Road
Donaghadee, Co. Down
N. Ireland, BT21 0NG**